EASTERN KENTUCKY PAPERS

In her dream Mrs. Wiley is shown Harman's Station

EASTERN KENTUCKY PAPERS

THE FOUNDING OF

HARMAN'S STATION

WITH AN ACCOUNT OF

THE INDIAN CAPTIVITY OF MRS. JENNIE WILEY AND THE EXPLORATION AND SETTLEMENT OF THE BIG SANDY VALLEY IN THE VIRGINIAS AND KENTUCKY

By WILLIAM ELSEY CONNELLEY

AUTHOR OF QUANTRILL AND THE BORDER WARS: THE HECKEWELDER NAR-
RATIVE: JOHN BROWN: WYANDOT FOLK-LORE: THE PROVI-
SIONAL GOVERNMENT OF NEBRASKA TERRITORY, ETC.

TO WHICH IS AFFIXED A BRIEF ACCOUNT OF THE CONNELLY
FAMILY AND SOME OF ITS COLLATERAL AND
RELATED FAMILIES IN AMERICA

NEW YORK
THE TORCH PRESS, 29-33 WEST 42D STREET
MDCCCCX

Facsimile Reprint

Published 1988 By

HERITAGE BOOKS INC.
1540E Pointer Ridge Place, Bowie, Maryland 20716
(301)-390-7709

ISBN 1-55613-168-2

A Complete Catalog Listing Hundreds Of Titles On
Genealogy, History, And Americana
Available Free Upon Request

THE TORCH PRESS
CEDAR RAPIDS
IOWA

PREFACE

The introductory chapter to the history of most of the early settlements of Kentucky is the story of a tragedy. In many instances this characteristic of their annals is repeated, often deepened and intensified, for a number of years after their beginning. This feature does not apply to the history of one locality more than to that of another. It is the general rule and is found in the story of almost every community. The founding of Harman's Station on the Louisa River[1] was directly caused by a tragedy as dark and horrible as any ever perpetrated by the savages upon the exposed and dangerous frontier of Virginia. The destruction of the home of Thomas Wiley in the valley of Walker's Creek, the murder of his children, the captivity of his wife by savages and her miraculous escape were the first incidents in a series of events in the history of Kentucky which properly belong to the annals of the Big Sandy Valley. Over them time has cast a tinge of romance, and they have grown in historical importance for more than a century. While they have been treasured by the people in that portion of Eastern Kentucky adjacent to the Virginias for more than a hundred years they

---

[1] *The Louisa River was named by Dr. Thomas Walker on Thursday, the 7th day of June, 1750. The entry in Dr. Walker's Journal describing this event is as follows: "June 7th. — The Creek being fordable, we Crossed it & kept down 12 miles to a River about 100 yards over, Which We called Louisa River. The Creek is about 30 yards wide, & part of ye River breaks into ye Creek — making an Island on which we Camped."*

In the early days of the settlement of the Big Sandy Valley this stream was known altogether as the Louisa River. As late as 1825 it was generally called the Louisa River. After that time, and to some extent before, the name began to be corrupted to that of Levisa. *The name* Levisa *is now used almost entirely. That the name is a corruption of the true name, Louisa,*

are preserved mainly in tradition. Indeed, it is to tradition principally that we must look for the sources of much of the history of all Eastern Kentucky. For the history of Kentucky, so far as it has been written at all, deals almost wholly with events which transpired in the "blue grass region" of the State.

Thirteen years after the establishment of the first permanent white settlement of Kentucky at Harrodsburg a strong healthy settlement of hardy, bold, self-reliant backwoodsmen was made in what is now Johnson County. Among the founders of this settlement were a number of the most noted explorers, scouts, guides, riflemen, and Indian fighters ever developed by the harsh and dangerous times of the frontier days of Virginia and the Carolinas. Why some substantial account of the station founded by these men in that wilderness was not made a matter of record by some historical writer of those times is one of the strange things occasionally found in the annals of a State. In the company which made this settlement were Matthias Harman, Henry Skaggs, James Skaggs, and Robert Hawes, all members of that famous party known in history as the Long Hunters. These and others of the company had been in the front ranks of those audacious rangers of the wilderness who wrested the Ohio Valley from its savage owners. Through this settlement they seized and finally held the valley of the Louisa River. The contest was desperate, and they were forced to abandon their station for a time by fierce and frequent attacks made upon it by the Indian tribes living beyond the Ohio,

there is no doubt. It appears that the name Louisa once attached to the whole State of Kentucky, but the extent of the application of this name is not now known. There is reason to believe that as early as 1775 the name Louisa was corrupted to Levisa. Speed, in the Wilderness Road, says "that Felix Walker, with Captain Twetty and six others, left Rutherford, North Carolina, in February 1775 (according to Felix Walker's narrative), 'to explore the country of Leowvisay, now Kentucky.'" But the u was formerly written v, and it may have been so in this word Leowvisay; in that case it would be Leowuisay, an erroneous spelling of Louisa.

The Kentucky River was sometimes called the Louisa River by the pioneers and explorers, and it was called, also, the Cherokee River. In the deed

who destroyed the blockhouse. But these courageous hunters returned with reinforcements and rebuilt their ruined fort never again to yield it to any foe. There most of them spent the remainder of their days, and there they lie buried. Descendants of many of them live in that country to this day.

It was distinctly remembered by many old people whom I knew in my youth that Matthias Harman in company with his kinsmen and other forest rangers established a hunting station and built a large cabin of logs, prior to the Sandy Creek Voyage, on the identical spot which afterwards became the site of their blockhouse. It is probable that this hunting lodge was the first log cabin built in what is now the State of Kentucky which came to be the basis of a permanent settlement of English-speaking people. The settlement made there was self-supporting. No government took any notice of its existence until it was firmly established. It did not cost the States of Virginia or Kentucky a farthing at any time. Not so much as a pound of powder or bar of lead was ever contributed by either State to its equipment or defense, although it was repeatedly raided by Indians and the fort fiercely attacked, once so persistently and with such force that, as said above, the settlers returned to Virginia for a short time.

I recognized the necessity for some reliable record of the historical events in the settlement of Eastern Kentucky while but yet a boy. Seeing that no man set his hand to the task, and believing it the duty of every one to labor for the common good as best he can, I began then to collect

from the Cherokees to Richard Henderson and others, proprietors of the Transylvania Company, conveying the tract of land known as the Great Grant, we find the description of the land beginning as follows: "All that tract, territory, or parcel of land, situated, lying and being in North America, on the Ohio River one of the eastern branches of the Mississippi River, beginning on the said Ohio, at the mouth of Kentucky, Cherokee, or what by the English is called Louisa River." This calling of the Kentucky River by the name Louisa was caused by a misapprehension. It was not certainly known what river had been called Louisa by Dr. Walker, as he traced none of the rivers, which he named, to the Ohio. But that he did not call the Kentucky River Louisa is shown by Lewis Evans's Map, 1775, on which the Louisa

and preserve such information pertaining to that subject as I could find. I knew personally many pioneers of that country; some of them were of my own family. Some of these old people could give little of value. Others could recite connected and interesting narratives covering the events of three-fourths of a century. Many of them had been through the stirring times of the early settlements made in the country about the New River and the head waters of the Clinch and the Holston. Of these events they told me.

Tradition alone does not constitute sufficient authority for positive historical statements. When, however, tradition is found well defined and uniform as to material facts throughout a large district it always preserves valuable material for the historian, and very frequently it is found to be more reliable than written annals. As a confirmatory medium it often renders the writer the highest service. In that capacity I have availed myself of its assistance in preparing this account of the founding of Harman's Station. The sources of my authority are far above mere traditional declarations. The pioneers gave me information of events of which they had, in many instances, personal knowledge, and all the events of which they spoke were so recent that their knowledge of them may properly be considered personal.

In all matters concerning Mrs. Jennie Wiley I have followed the account given me by her son, Adam P. Wiley. There are several reasons why I have adhered to his statements in that matter. I knew him intimately and long,

River is marked as flowing into the Great Kanawha, and the upper course of the "Tottery or Big Sandy C." is marked "Frederick R." Frederick's River was discovered and named by Dr. Walker on the 2d of June, 1750, five days before he discovered and named the Louisa River, and as it is now known that the Louisa River does not flow into the Great Kanawha, it follows that the west branch of the Big Sandy River was the stream upon which Dr. Walker bestowed the name Louisa.

Rev. Zephaniah Meek wrote me from Catlettsburg, Kentucky, November 19, 1895, as follows: "I called on Capt. Owens yesterday, formerly of Pike county, and asked him the origin of the name Levisa as applied to the west fork of the Big Sandy. He says that in the early settlement of this part of

and I never heard his reputation for truth and veracity brought into question. He was a minister of the Gospel. His mind was a storehouse of history and border story. He possessed fine oratorical and conversational powers. His memory was wonderful and it was not impaired by the great age to which he lived. He was thirty-three when his mother died. His opportunity for exact knowledge of what did actually transpire was far superior to that of any other pioneer living into my generation. When I saw him last he was past eighty, but he was erect and only slightly gray. He knew personally a number of the Long Hunters. He knew the Ingles family and could give a better account of the captivity and escape of Mrs. Mary Ingles than I have ever found in any published work. He was perfectly familiar with the topography of all the country over which his mother was carried captive, and this enabled him to identify localities and make his narrative complete and explicit. It is possible he may have been in error in some minor matters. It was long my opinion that Mrs. Wiley could not have marched to the Tug River in the time allowed by Mr. Wiley. But he insisted that he was right, and knowing the iron endurance of the pioneer men and women it came to be my conviction that Mrs. Wiley did make this march in the time stated. I was doubtful, too, of the ability of the Indians to cross the Tug and the Louisa rivers with Mrs. Wiley in the manner described by Mr. Wiley. Since then, however, I have become well acquainted with members of the Wyandot, Shawnee, Delaware, and Cherokee tribes, and have seen them per-

---

the State, a French trader by the name of Le Visa came to what is now Louisa, and owing to some experiences of his, that fork came to be called after his name, hence, Americanized Levisa.''

There may have been a French trader at the forks of the Big Sandy by the name of Le Visa, but the word of Captain Owens is all the evidence I have found of that fact. If there was such a trader he was not prominent enough to change the name of a river or to have his name attach to it. The i in French is e in English. Anglicized, the Frenchman's name would have been Levesay or Levesy. Levisa could not possibly have come from it. The explanation of Captain Owens is a very improbable one.

John P. Hale, in his Trans-Allegheny Pioneers says: '' The La Visa, or

form feats in swiftly running water much more marvelous than that pictured by Mr. Wiley. In the matter of dates I have invariably followed Mr. Wiley. I believe it was sound judgment to do so. There are many circumstances to corroborate him, among the strongest being the mention of Harman's Station in the map published by Imlay in 1793.

Mr. Wiley was very anxious that the exact account of his mother's captivity and escape should be preserved. Although deficient in the matter of education he did try more than once to write it out. So unsatisfactory were his efforts that he did not preserve them. He exacted from me a promise that I would write the account of the trials and sufferings of his mother. This is the fulfilment of that promise. I have performed the work to the best of my ability. I believe there will be found no great errors, though I realize that I may have fallen into minor mistakes. If it should turn out so, I am confident any fault discovered will prove unimportant and immaterial.

Mrs. Wiley has many descendants living in Kentucky and West Virginia. The Indians murdered her brother and five of her children. After her return from captivity to her husband there were five children born to them— Hezekiah, Jane, Sarah, Adam, and William.

Hezekiah married Christine Nelson, of Lawrence County; moved to Wayne County, West Virginia, and settled on Twelve Pole Creek; died near his old home while on a visit, in 1882.

Levisa, fork is said to mean the picture, design, or representation. It was so called by an early French explorer in that region, from Indian pictures or signs, painted on trees, near the head of the stream.''

These painted trees were to be found in early times all along the Louisa River from the mouth of Big Paint Creek, where they were most numerous, to its head. Christopher Gist was on the Pound River in 1751. The entry in his Journal for Wednesday, April 3, is as follows: '' . . . to a small Creek on which was a large Warriors camp, that would contain 70 or 80 Warriors, their Captains Name or Title was the Crane, as I knew by his Picture or Arms painted on a tree.'' Darlington says: ''This was on the stream called Indian Creek, the middle fork of the Big Sandy, in Wise

Jane married Richard Williamson; also settled on Twelve Pole Creek; died there.

Sarah married first Christian Yost; moved to Wayne County, West Virginia. There, after the death of her first husband, she married Samuel Murray; died March 10, 1871.

Both Adam and William left families in Johnson County, Kentucky.

The full name of Adam was Adam Prevard Wiley. Prevard *was a mispronunciation of* Brevard. *Mrs. Wiley was related by blood to the North Carolina family of that name. That is why she gave the name to her son. The name was often erroneously written* Prevard, *and even* Pervard.

Mr. Wiley gave Matthias Harman due credit for intelligent leadership as this work will show. He believed few men on the border ever equaled Matthias Harman in Indian warfare and woodcraft.

Like all people who dwell in rural communities Mr. Wiley kept himself well informed on all subjects of local lore. He knew the locality from which almost every family had emigrated to Kentucky, and he knew what families had intermarried both before and after they left Virginia. He knew the number of children of most of the pioneers, their names, and when they were born. To this day when a number of Big Sandy Valley people meet they discuss the intermarriages of various families of their acquaintance, when they occurred, when and where the contracting parties were born, where the families came from to Ken-

County. *The Crane was a totem or badge of one of the Miami tribes; also of the Wyandots. A common practice among the Indian tribes, with war parties at a distance from home, was to paint on trees or a rock figures of warriors, prisoners, animals, etc., as intelligible to other Indians as a printed handbill among the whites."* Darlington *is in error when he says there was a totem of the Crane among the Wyandots. But they had a chief named Tarhe, or the Crane, who was old enough in 1751 to have led a hunting party or even a war party into the wilderness. He became head chief of the Wyandots on the death of the Half King.*

It might be possible that these many paintings suggested to some of the early explorers and hunters some such name for this stream as Device Fork,

tucky, and every other feature of the matter. The work on the history of the Big Sandy Valley by Dr. William Ely is made up of family genealogies. Rev. M. T. Burris wrote for me a manuscript of almost one hundred pages on the history of the Valley; nine-tenths of it is genealogy. I have been collecting information along that same line for forty years and am still at it. I believe I have material from which can be constructed a genealogical record of the people of that valley which will be more complete than can possibly be made of any other district in America of equal age and area.

This is a beginning in the work of writing the history of Eastern Kentucky. I am confident that no other part of the State has a more interesting history than that of the Big Sandy Valley. When the full record is made up it will show that Eastern Kentucky was settled almost exclusively by men who served in the patriot armies of the Revolution, and that no other community of equal size had so great a proportion of those heroic men. I mention that fact at this time because malice and ignorance in the ''blue grass region'' delight to speak in disparaging terms of the ancestry of the mountaineer. The blood of the mountaineer is the purest on the continent, and his language is the purest Anglo-Saxon speech to be found in America.

William Elsey Connelley

816 Lincoln Street, Topeka, Kansas,
July 7, 1910

---

or Device River, or Devices Fork, or Devices River, *and that such name or names finally assumed the form of Levisa Fork, etc. This is only suggested as a remotely possible origin of the name* Levisa. *It is far-fetched; there is no probability at all that such is the origin of the name. That* Levisa *is a corruption of* Louisa *may be accepted as beyond dispute or question.*

Dr. Walker *gave this river the name* Louisa *in honor of* Louisa, *the wife of the Duke of Cumberland, it is said. Louisa is a good old English name, coming down from a more ancient people. It is a name of much beauty, and it was in great favor with our ancestors. It should be restored to the river to which Dr. Walker gave it. The Louisa Fork should be called the Louisa River. The Tug Fork should be called the Tug River. The river formed by their junction should be called the Big Sandy River.*

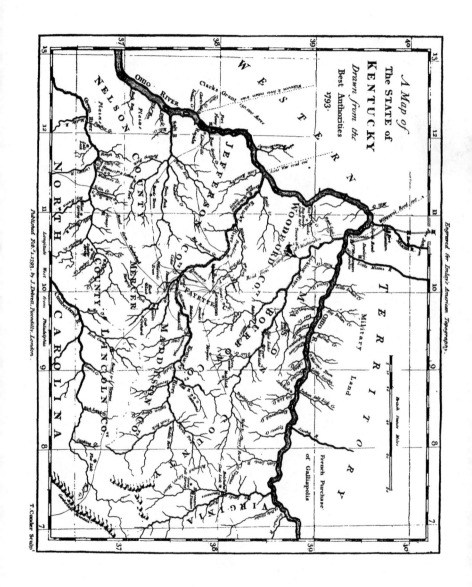

A Map of
The STATE of
KENTUCKY
Drawn from the
Best Authorities
1793.

TABLE OF CONTENTS

MAPS AND ILLUSTRATIONS

CHAPTER I

By virtue of conquest the Iroquois claimed all the country between the Ohio and the Tennessee. They could not themselves occupy the land they had conquered. Other tribes stood in terror of them and did not encroach upon the territory to which they laid claim. Consequently few aboriginal settlements were found in what is now the State of Kentucky. Alien tribes seem to have roamed over it in search of game. Hostile nations sometimes met in the gloom of its great forests in deadly conflict. It came to be regarded as the common battle ground. In time the Cherokees formulated a shadowy claim to a portion of it which they disposed of to Henderson and his associates. This gave the English an ambiguous title to the soil which was never relinquished, although the French appealed to arms in contention for possession of the Ohio Valley. The defeat of Braddock left the English frontiers without protection from savage bands. Frequent and bloody invasions followed, and these were not ended by the final triumph of the English. The French inhabitants of Canada passed under the dominion of a government against which they bore the deepest enmity. The result was the Conspiracy of Pontiac, which carried the torch, the tomahawk, and the scalping-knife into the frontier settlements from Pennsylvania to Georgia. Painted warriors lurked on the skirts of every frontier community, save for brief intermissions, for the next thirty years. Blazing cabin-homes in the red glare of which lay murdered and scalped families, captive wives and daughters led away into the wilderness to degradation worse than death, fathers and sons tortured at the stake — these were common occurrences all along the western borders of the English settlements until the peace of Greenville in 1795.

To oppose, and, so far as possible, to prevent these atrocities, and to occasionally perpetrate similar or more horrible ones upon the Indians, there was developed that class of hardy backwoodsmen, hunters, adventurers, riflemen, and forest-rangers who traversed the wilderness beyond the confines of civilization and afforded what protection they could to the exposed and defenseless pioneers.[2]

In 1763 the line defining the frontier extended from Ingles's Ferry on the New River to the Susquehanna. It followed along the crest of that range of the Alleghanies which separates the waters of the Ohio from the head branches of the Potomac and the James. Fort Pitt was an outpost far beyond the remotest settlements. A few pioneers were to be found on the head waters of the Monongahela and other tributaries of the Ohio.[3] South and southwest from Ingles's Ferry there were at that time no settlements of English-speaking folk west of the Alleghanies on the borders of Virginia or the Carolinas. A chance settler or an occasional hunter, all trace of whom is now

---

[2] "They were a distinct, peculiar class, marked with striking contrasts of good and evil. Many, though by no means all, were coarse, audacious and unscrupulous; yet even in the worst, one might often have found a vigorous growth of warlike virtues, an iron endurance, an undespairing courage, a wondrous sagacity, and singular fertility of resource. In them was renewed, with all its ancient energy, that wild and daring spirit, that force and hardihood of mind, which marked our barbarous ancestors of Germany and Norway."— Parkman, *Conspiracy of Pontiac*, Vol. I, p. 158.

[3] In his Journal Dr. Thomas Walker mentions one Samuel Stalnacker whom he assisted to build a house on the Holston River in 1750. He seems to have been an Indian trader and to have been in this region for a number of years previous to that date; but the house he built in 1750 never, so far as we know, became the nucleus of any permanent community. One James McCall is also mentioned by Dr. Walker as living west of the New River in 1750. A colony of "Duncards" lived on the west bank of the New River at Ingles's Ferry in 1750, so Dr. Walker says in his Journal.

lost to us, may previously have taken up his abode in those regions. To the line indicated the vanguard of the English advance had pushed. Beyond lay the wilderness, deep, dark, dangerous, unexplored, unknown, but with a fascination wholly irresistible. Mongrel hordes of painted savages wandered through its forest reaches in search of the buffalo, the deer, the bear, and often in stealthy and deadly search for one another.

Here was a land having the inherent capacity for the development and maintenance of an empire unpeopled and wrapped in the unbroken silence of perpetual solitude. It was a desirable land, a land of plenty for even barbarians. Food was easily obtained by them, for unnumbered thousands of the American bison congregated on the treeless plains of the Illinois and the Ohio, and herds of deer wandered in the sunless mazes of the forest-clad ranges of the Cumberland and the Alleghanies. It was a land of enchanting beauty. Savage tribes of barbarians contended for it. The contumelious Frenchman buried leaden plates upon the wooded shores of its principal rivers in defiant challenge to the further advance of the stubborn Briton who was slowly but irresistibly pushing deeper and deeper into it from his compact habitat along the Atlantic seaboard with the immutable purposes of conquest and occupancy.

CHAPTER II

Hezekiah Sellards was a Scotch-Irish pioneer in the Upper Shenandoah Valley. He moved into that country from Pennsylvania. He built his cabin twenty miles from the nearest neighbor. He was a typical settler and a genuine frontiersman and backwoodsman. The location of his residence in the Valley cannot now be determined with any degree of certainty. It was in the mountains about the sources of the Shenandoah River. It was in a community where many Presbyterians afterward settled. Sellards himself was a Presbyterian of the strictest sort. He was a man of strong character and sterling worth. He was of such standing in his church that in the absence of the minister he could hold the services, and he often preached to congregations which assembled in his house upon his invitation. For his time and place he was a man of considerable property, industry, economy and thrift being strong characteristics of the old woodsman. He was a man of some learning, and at considerable trouble and expense he had his children instructed in the common elementary branches. His children were strictly trained in that severity of morals exacted of the old Covenanters. These religious principles were the foundation upon which they were expected to build correct lives.

The above makes up the sum total of what is known of Hezekiah Sellards in his residence on the Shenandoah. In addition to his farming he was a hunter. In company with his neighbors he made annual journeys into forests beyond the New River. The object of the hunter in those days was as much to find a desirable place in which to locate when next he determined to move as to secure meat

The Sellards Colony moving from the Shenandoah Valley to Walker's Creek

and skins. A more charming country than the western highlands of Virginia would be difficult indeed to find. Sellards and his associates hunted in that region about the head of Wolf Creek, and along Walker's Creek, going sometimes to the Clinch and the Holston. Their choice of locality finally fell upon Walker's Creek and Walker's Mountain. Long before it was safe to do so, perhaps before 1760, a colony of which Sellards was a member and perhaps the leader settled about Walker's Mountain. The date is not definite, but they were beset by Indians for thirty years. In their migration to their new home they drove their flocks and herds before them and carried their wives and children and their household effects upon pack-horses.

The names of the other families of this western migration are not now positively known. It is probable that the Staffords, Porters, Damrons, and others now represented in the Eastern Kentucky families came into that part of Virginia with Hezekiah Sellards. The number of persons and families cannot now be told, but prudence demanded that settlers going into the wilderness should go in sufficient force to withstand the Indian bands by which they were sure to be assailed. Sellards and his associates conformed to the type found all along the frontier. They were soldiers as well as settlers. They were armed with the old, long, heavy, hair-trigger, flint-lock rifle, and with that rude weapon their aim was true and deadly. In woodcraft they could circumvent the Indian. They were cool, positive, confident, alert, courageous, resourceful, and self-reliant.

Before going on with the work in hand it will be profitable to note a few features of backwoods life. The pioneers were their own tanners, harness-makers and shoemakers. They built their own houses and made their own furniture and agricultural implements. Salt and iron were indispensable and had to be brought in upon pack-horses from the stations or older settlements where they were purchased with skins, furs, dried venison, and ginseng. Both were used sparingly. Often a cabin was completed without there being a single nail, bolt, or spike used in its construction. Flax and cotton were grown by almost every settler. These with the wool from the few sheep that escaped the wolves furnished material for cloth which was woven in looms in the pioneer homes. The feathers of ducks and geese furnished beds which found so much favor that they have not been discarded to this day. Clothing for the women was home spun, home woven, and home made, coarse, but substantial and comfortable. That of the men was of the same manufacture and often supplemented with skins, dressed and not dressed. The fringed hunting-shirt and leggins, fur cap and moccasins, made a picturesque garb, and for the scout, guide, hunter, trapper, explorer, or any other dweller in the wilderness it was the most appropriate that could have been devised.

For food the pioneer depended upon Indian corn, his hogs, and the fruits of the chase. The cornfields surrounded every cabin. Bacon was the favorite meat. Vegetables and fruits grew quickly and of fine quality; many edible fruits were found growing wild. Coffee was unknown, and tea was unheard of; substitutes were made from spicewood and sassafras. Chickens, turkeys, ducks, and geese were found about most cabins.

The division of labor was not so distinct as it is now. Women often worked in the field, plied the axe, sheared the sheep, pulled the flax, plucked the feathers from the geese and ducks and frequently did effective service with the rifle. These things were in addition to their ordinary work of preparing food, spinning and dyeing thread and yarn, weaving cloth therefrom, making the clothing, and attending to many other affairs amid all the cares and anxieties incident to rearing large families on an exposed and dangerous frontier.[4]

---

[4] The manner of living here described had not entirely changed in Eastern Kentucky even in 1875. Many of the features here described remained in the home of my grandfather, Henry Connelly, Esq., who lived on the Middle Fork of Jennie's Creek, Johnson County, until his death in 1877. Most of the cloth for the clothing of himself and his family was made by my aunts from cotton, flax and wool produced on his farm. I often assisted in this manufacture when a child. I could spin on the " big wheel," fill the " quills " for the shuttles used in weaving, and I have " reeled " thread and yarn, much against my will, sometimes, I must say, until my arms ached. My grandfather raised on his farm his own corn and wheat. He raised cattle, hogs, and horses. He cured his own bacon and dried and cured his own beef. He manufactured most of the agricultural implements used on his farm. He had large orchards. For more than forty years he made his own sugar from the maples growing on his land. He manufactured his own cheese. He was an industrious and independent American citizen, and his manner of life was the best. A return to it by the people would solve many serious questions now troubling the Republic.

CHAPTER III

Hezekiah Sellards had a large family, but all his children save four died before they were grown up. Two of his sons, Thomas and Jack, lived on the Buffalo Fork of John's Creek and died there, each at a great age.[5] One daughter married John Borders, a British soldier who served under Cornwallis and was captured at Yorktown. During his service he had come to believe in America and in her cause and had resolved to make this country his home as soon as he could secure his discharge from the army. It is said that he had acquainted his officers of his intention. After the surrender of Cornwallis Borders soon contrived to be released, and he went immediately to the back settlements of Virginia to begin life in his adopted country. There he met and married a daughter of Hezekiah Sellards. He was an excellent man in every respect, so it is said. From his marriage with Miss Sellards are descended several families living now in Eastern Kentucky, one of the most numerous and respectable being that of Borders.[6]

The remaining daughter of Hezekiah Sellards was Jean, familiarly called by her family and others Jennie Sellards. Her son informed me that she had black hair through which ran a tinge of auburn in her youth. Others say her

---

[5] Stated on the authority of Adam P. Wiley, also Rev. M. T. Burris, now of Golden, Mo. Mr. Burris writes me that he knew these brothers. He was born and brought up in the Leslie Settlement on John's Creek, and is a descendant of the pioneer Leslie.

[6] The descendants of John Borders live now mainly in Lawrence and Johnson counties, Kentucky. They are scattered over all the Mississippi Valley. While many of them were farmers, they usually followed commercial life and were very successful.

hair was coal black, and they saw her many times and had
opportunity to know. All agree that she was strong and
capable of great exertion and great endurance. Until past
middle life she was of fine form and her movements were
quick. In her old age she became heavy and slow. She
had then, too, heavy overhanging brows. Her eyes were
black. She was above medium height. Her face was
agreeable and indicated superior intelligence. She was
persistent and determined in any matter she had decided
to accomplish. She labored in her father's fields. She
was familiar with every feature of woodcraft and was a
splendid shot with the rifle; even after she settled in the
Big Sandy Valley it required an expert to equal her. Before her marriage she had killed bears, wolves, panthers
and other wild animals. She was at home in the woods
and could hold her way over the trails of the country
either by day or by night. She was endowed with an
abundance of good hard Scotch common-sense. In spinning, weaving, and other work of the household she was
proficient. I have set down what her son said about her.
Most of it was confirmed by other witnesses. Her son insisted that until age began to tell on her she was a handsome woman.[7]

Captain Matthias Harman lived on Walker's Creek and
not a great distance from Hezekiah Sellards. He was
familiar with all the country along the frontier and this

[7] Rev. M. T. Burris says "she was rather dark skinned, dark hair
and heavy eye bones." He also says that Thomas Lewis, a pioneer in
the Big Sandy Valley who knew Mrs. Wiley well, told him that she "had
dark hair, rather heavy eyebones, and dark eyebrows." Joseph Kelley
was also a pioneer in the Big Sandy Valley and knew Mrs. Wiley well; he
told Mr. Burris that she had dark hair. Mr. Burris says that her brothers,
Thomas and Jack Sellards, had black or dark hair. Mr. Burris did not
know Mrs. Wiley. Adam P. Wiley was dark of skin, and his hair was
black. My great grandmother, Mrs. Susan Connelly, knew Mrs. Wiley well;
she told me that Mrs. Wiley had very dark hair, was tall, handsome form
and face until old age made her heavy and slow, very intelligent, kindly
disposition but firm and determined, and a devout and earnest Christian

brought his services into demand by persons seeking new
lands suitable for settlements. It is said that in the spring
if 1777 he led a number of settlers from Strasburg, Virginia, to Ab's Valley. Thomas and Samuel Wiley were
members of this party. They were brothers, recently arrived from the north of Ireland. Samuel Wiley settled in
Ab's Valley, but Thomas remained at the home of Captain
Harman, of whom he finally purchased a tract of land.
This tract of land was on a branch of Walker's Creek immediately north of the residence of Harman. Wiley built
a cabin of two rooms with an open space between on his
land and cleared a field. He courted Jennie Sellards and
met with many a rebuff from her father whose hostility
availed nothing, for Jennie looked with favor on the young
man and they were married. This was in the year 1779.

There is nothing in the life of Thomas Wiley and his
wife essential to this account the first few years of their
married life. They labored to raise corn and other crops.
Cows and pigs were among their possessions. Wiley did
not become a good hunter, but he ranged the woods in
search of ginseng. Children were born to them. They
lived the simple lives of pioneers as did their neighbors.
And their neighbors were few and far between.

It is necessary here to return to the transactions of
Matthias Harman.[8] Mention has been already made of
the colony located by him in the vicinity of Ab's Valley.

[8] Matthias Harman was born in or near Strasburg, Virginia, about
the year 1732.   His father, Heinrich Herrmann, came from Prussia
to Pennsylvania, it is said, and from thence to the vicinity of Strasburg
while yet a young man. Matthias Harman and his brothers, of whom he
had several, early became hunters and ranged the woods far and near.
They joined every expedition into the wilderness made up in their community, and it is said that their father also joined these expeditions,
whether for hunting, exploration, or for war. The Harmans bore the Indian a bitter hatred and believed in his extermination. There came to
America also, two brothers of Heinrich Herrmann, Adam and Jacob, but
they came at a later date. These three brothers and their families were
among the first settlers at Draper's Meadows in 1748. Michael Steiner or
Stoner, was a cousin to Matthias Harman, and was also an early settler at

The Wiley Cabin on Walker's Creek. Drawn from description given by Adam P. Wiley

He made a number of such settlements in the country west of the New River. It had been for thirty years his intention to make a settlement at the mouth of John's Creek on the Louisa River when the attitude of the Indians would permit him to do so with safety. The Indian tribes beyond the Ohio and the Cherokees living along the Little Tennessee had all to be taken into account. Some vagrant bands of Cherokees lived also along the Ohio River at the time. Harman was infatuated with the Louisa River country because game was more plentiful there than in any other region of which he knew. The great Indian trails between the Ohio River Indians and the Cherokees and other southern tribes lay up the Big Sandy, which accounts for the fact that the Indians roamed that country several years after they had disappeared from all other parts of Kentucky. For this colony Harman had enlisted a number of his old-time associates and companions in wilderness exploration. In 1787 he believed it safe to

Draper's Meadows. It is said that Casper Mansker, the famous pioneer of Tennessee, was in some degree related to the Harmans. These men were called Dutchmen by the early settlers. They were all explorers of the wilderness, and hunting became a passion with them. Matthias Harman became infatuated with the life of the woodsman and the dangers of the frontier. In woodcraft and Indian warfare it is doubtful if he ever had a superior. He was one of the men employed to guide the Sandy Creek Voyage, and tradition says that if General Lewis had been governed by his judgment the expedition would not have failed of its purpose. He and his Dutch companions and relatives slew about forty Cherokees who were returning home from assisting the English against Fort Du Quesne in 1758, so tradition in the Harman family says, and they justified their action by affirming that the Indians had stolen horses and cattle from the settlers along their route. Tradition in the Big Sandy Valley said that Michael Stoner and Casper Mansker were with Harman in this foray, and that the party received pay from the colony of Virginia for the scalps of the Indians slain and that it amounted to a considerable sum per man.

These Germans and explorers with whom they were associated became familiar with every part of the Big Sandy Valley soon after settling at Draper's Meadows. They built a lodge or hunters' cabin on the Louisa River just below the mouth of John's Creek about the year 1755, and they went there to hunt the deer, elk, buffalo, bear, beaver, and other game animals and birds every year. Matthias Harman appears to have been the

establish his settlement, and it was agreed that it should be made in the winter of 1787-88.

Harman's father was yet living. He always went with the other pioneers to hunt in the Big Sandy Valley. Except for a few years during the Revolution this hunt had been made annually for twenty five years and perhaps longer. As the hunters would not return when they went out in the fall of 1787, and as Harman, senior, was now too old to go with the colony and was desirous of making a hunt with his sons this year it was arranged that a party would go out for a few weeks prior to the departure to build the fort on the Louisa. Where the hunters made their camp cannot now be determined. It was not far from the settlements, and it appears to have been near the head waters of both the Tug and Louisa rivers. It is said that about twenty hunters went out in this party. Henry Harman and his sons, Henry Skaggs, James Skaggs, Robert

---

leader. Associated with him were Henry Skaggs and James Skaggs, famous hunters and explorers.

Matthias Harman was called '' Tice '' or '' Tias '' Harman by his companions. He was diminutive in size, in height being but little more than five feet, and his weight never exceeded one hundred and twenty pounds. He had an enormous nose and a thin sharp face. He had an abundance of hair of a yellow tinge, beard of a darker hue, blue eyes which anger made green and glittering, and a bearing bold and fearless. He possessed an iron constitution, and could endure more fatigue and privation than any of his associates. He was a dead shot with the long rifle of his day. The Indians believed him in league with the devil or some other malevolent power because of their numbers he killed, his miraculous escapes, and the bitterness and relentless daring of his warfare against them. He was one of the Long Hunters, as were others of the Harmans, and more than once did his journeys into the wilderness carry him to the Mississippi River. He and the other Harmans able to bear arms were in the Virginia service in the War of the Revolution. He is said to have formed the colony which made the first settlement in Ab's Valley. He formed the colony which made the first settlement in Eastern Kentucky and erected the blockhouse. He brought in the settlers who rebuilt the blockhouse, and for a number of years he lived in the Blockhouse Bottom or its vicinity. In his extreme old age he returned to Virginia and died there. It is said he lived to be ninety-six, but I have not the date or place of his death.

The Battle with the Indians at the Hunting Camp, in which Matthias Harman killed the son of the Cherokee Chief

Hawes, some of the Damrons, and a man named Draper are known to have been of the party that went on this preliminary hunt.

As it was the intention of the hunters to remain some time in the woods they built a rough camp in which to sleep and to shelter their trappings in case of rain. The camp must have been near the Indian highway, for one day it was surprised and attacked by a roving band of Indians. Few particulars of this skirmish have been preserved, though the memory of it is widespread. It is said that the previous night had been rainy and the morning cloudy and damp. The men had not gone out early, and that fortunate circumstance saved the camp from destruction, in all probability. The hunters not being beyond hearing of gunshots returned at once, catching the Indian party in the rear and defeating the savages in a short time. Robert Hawes was wounded in one of his arms. The Indians were pressing the party at the camp when the other hunters returned. A young Cherokee, son of the chief and leader, was armed with bow and arrows only, but he came near killing Henry Harman and would possibly have done so had not Matthias Harman killed him with a rifle shot. The death of the Indian boy ended the fight. The chief carried the body of his son away with him. Matthias Harman recognized the Cherokee chief as one of the boldest raiders on the Virginia settlements to be found in all the tribes. He stole horses all along the frontier, murdered families, and carried off plunder of all kinds. Harman had followed him often and had met him in many a running fight. A bitter hatred existed between the two men, and the Cherokee had tried to destroy Harman's family several times when Harman was engaged in scouting and was absent from home, but his attempts had never been successful; he had frequently driven off horses and cattle belonging to Harman. It is said that Harman and

this chief had been friends at one time, and that they were
both guides in the Sandy Creek Voyage.[9]

When the Indians disappeared Matthias Harman determined to return home at once. He was certain that the
Cherokee would fall upon the settlements and inflict what
damage he could, for he was a daring marauder and is
represented to have been persistent in the pursuit of re-

---

[9] The traditionary accounts of this Indian attack vary much. In some
of them little of what actually happened can be found. H. C. Ragland, of
Logan, West Virginia, confuses it with the Sandy Creek Voyage. Matthias
Harman, a nephew of the fourth generation from his famous uncle, for
whom he was named, wrote me the following:

"William Harman and Aquilla Harman were once out hunting on a
very cold day and the Indians made a raid upon the settlement in the
Baptist Valley [and] about this time or 1780 gave the settlers some
trouble. Henry Harman and his three sons, George Harman, Ed. Harman,
Tias Harman, and a man by the name of Draper followed them down the
Tug Fork of Sandy to what is now Warfield where they found the Indians
camped by a log and Harman fired on them. Draper left them.

"The Indians shot the old man Harman in the breast with arrow spikes
until he could not stand without leaning against a tree. His son, George,
loaded his gun for him. There he stood until he shot six of the Indians
dead. The seventh was wounded, ran into the Tug River and drowned
himself."

Rev. M. T. Burris included the following account in the manuscript he
prepared for me:

"Daniel Harman was a brother of Henry, George and Matthias Harman, the great Indian fighters and early explorers of Tug and Levisa Fork
of Big Sandy. They had a terrible battle with Indians on Tug River, up
near the Va. line. They came upon the Indians a little unexpected, George
Harman commanded his squad, and the battle opened in earnest, it seemed
at first that the Indians would be too much for them; Harman's boys said
to him, 'Had we not better retreat and try to save ourselves?' (A man
by the name of Draper ran at the first fire.) Harman replied in a determined voice, 'No! give them h—l! When you see me fall it will be
time to retreat.' At that word the boys took fresh courage and loaded
and kept blazing away. G. Harman was a brave man; the chief ran up
close to him, made motions to Harman to throw down his gun so he could
take him a prisoner but he would not, they closed in a scuffle, they were so
near equally yoked in strength the Indian could not hold him down; in
[the] scuffle Harman got hold of the Indian's butcher knife that was in
his belt, and began to use it in earnest, having the Indian by the legs, Indian's head down, biting Harman's legs. Harman stabbed him 24 times
before he dispatched him, the others took to their heels, as the Harman
company was proving too much for them. The Harmans had a rock [house]

venge, which it was believed he would now seek for his son slain in battle. The absence of Harman and other riflemen from the settlements gave him an opportunity which the hunters believed he would not let pass.

A number of arrowheads remained in the wounds of Henry Harman, making his condition serious. On this account no pursuit of the Indians was attempted. A litter

or cave in that region where they camped when on Tug, hunting and exploring. (These facts I learned from Adam Harman).''

Adam Harman, here mentioned by Mr. Burris, was a nephew in the third generation, of Matthias Harman. While there is much error in these meager accounts, they evidently preserve some of the details of the battle between the hunters and the Indians. I heard many such accounts as those quoted above. The one written in the text was given me by Adam P. Wiley. There were some things of which he was uncertain, and my description of the encounter is deficient in the matter of detail. But I wrote down all that I was certain of.

It is believed that this battle with the Indians by Harman and his sons and others was in fact that which is described by Bickley in his *History of Tazewell County, Virginia.* Adam P. Wiley said that Bickley had this battle in mind when he wrote his account, and that he was in error in many things, particularly the date, locality, the number of persons engaged on each side, and the important developments which grew out of it.

The late Dr. Witten, of Oklahoma City, Oklahoma, knew Bickley, and was in Tazewell County when his history was published. I have seen a letter from him to his son, T. A. Witten, Esq., a lawyer in Missouri, saying that Bickley fell into a good many errors, and that these were pointed out by the people there upon the appearance of the book. The same letter is authority for the assurance that Bickley was conscientious, and that the errors in his book were the result of insufficient research and investigation. He places the battle in 1784 and makes nothing of it more than an insignificant collision of stragglers, while in fact it was an important meeting of those contesting for the supremacy of the wilderness. I give his account:

'' In the fall of 1784, Henry Harman and his two sons, George and Matthias, and George Draper, left the settlement to engage in a bear hunt on Tug River. They were provided with pack-horses, independent of those used for riding, and on which were to be brought in the game. The country in which their hunt was to take place was penetrated by the ' war-path ' leading to and from the Ohio River; but as it was late in the season, they did not expect to meet with Indians.

'' Arriving at the hunting-grounds in the early part of the evening, they stopped and built their camp; a work executed generally by the old man, who might be said to be particular in having it constructed to his own taste. George and Matthias loaded and put their guns in order, and started to the woods to look for sign, and perchance to kill a buck for the

was made and the wounded man was sent to his home, which was in the vicinity of Ab's Valley, so it is said.

The surmise of the hunters concerning the intention of the Cherokee chief proved correct. He went as directly to Walker's Creek as he could from the battlefield. It was the judgment of the hunters afterwards when all the facts were known that he divided his band and sent a part

---

evening repast, while Draper busied himself in hobbling and caring for the horses.

" In a short time George returned with the startling intelligence of Indians. He had found a camp but a short distance from their own, in which the partly consumed sticks were still burning. They could not, of course, be at any considerable distance and might now be concealed near them, watching their every movement. George, while at the camp, had made a rapid search for sign, and found a pair of leggins, which he showed the old man. Now, old Mr. Harman was a type of frontiersman, in some things, and particularly that remarkable self-possession, which is so often to be met with in new countries, where dangers are ever in the path of the settler. So taking a seat on the ground, he began to interrogate his son on the dimensions, appearance, &c., of the camp. When he had fully satisfied himself, he remarked, that ' there must be from five to seven Indians,' and that they must pack up and hurry back to the settlement, to prevent, if possible, the Indians from doing mischief; and, said he, '*If we fall in with them we must fight them.*'

" Matthias was immediately called in, and the horses packed. Mr. Harman and Draper now began to load their guns, when the old man observing Draper laboring under what is known among hunters as the ' Buck ague,' being that state of excitement which causes excessive trembling, remarked to him, ' My son, I fear you cannot fight.'

" The plan of march was now agreed upon, which was, that Mr. Harman and Draper should lead the way, the pack-horses follow them, and Matthias and George bring up the rear. After they had started, Draper remarked to Mr. Harman, that he would get ahead, as he could see better than Mr. Harman, and that he would keep a sharp lookout. It is highly probable that he was cogitating a plan of escape, as he had not gone far before he declared he saw the Indians, which proved not to be true. Proceeding a short distance further, he suddenly wheeled his horse about, at the same time crying out, ' Yonder they are — behind that log.' As a liar is not to be believed, even when he speaks the truth, so Mr. Draper was not believed this time. Mr. Harman rode on, while a large dog he had with him, ran up to the log and reared himself upon it, showing no signs of the presence of Indians. At this second a sheet of fire and smoke from the Indian rifles, completely concealed the log from view, for Draper had really spoken the truth.

" Before the smoke had cleared away, Mr. Harman and his sons were dismounted, while Draper had fled with all the speed of a swift horse. There were seven of the Indians, only four of whom had guns; the rest being armed with bows and arrows, tomahawks and scalping-knives. As soon as they fired, they rushed on Mr. Harman, who fell back to where his sons stood ready to meet the Indians.

" They immediately surrounded the three white men, who had formed a triangle, each looking out, or, what would have been, with men enough, a hollow square. The old gentleman bid Matthias to reserve his fire, while himself and George fired, wounding, as it would seem, two of the Indians.

of it on to the Cherokee towns, perhaps with the body of
his son. The hunters believed there were more Indians
in the party which attacked their camp than in the band
which fell upon the home of Thomas Wiley. It was known
later that the party with which the Cherokee attacked the
settlement was composed of two Cherokees, three Shawnees, three Wyandots, three Delawares, a total of eleven
Indians — a mongrel band, a thing not uncommon at that

George was a lame man, from having had white swelling in his childhood,
and after firing a few rounds, the Indians noticed his limping, and one
who had fired at him, rushed upon him, thinking him wounded. George
saw the fatal tomahawk raised, and drawing his gun, prepared to
meet it. When the Indian had got within striking distance, George let
down upon his head with the gun, which brought him to the ground; he
soon recovered and made at him again, half bent and head foremost, intending, no doubt, to trip him up. But as he got near enough, George
sprang up and jumped across him, which brought the Indian to his knees.
Feeling for his own knife, and not getting hold of it, he seized the Indian's
and plunged it deep into his side. Matthias struck him on the head with
a tomahawk, and finished the work with him.

"Two Indians had attacked the old man with bows, and were maneuver-
ing around him, to get a clear fire at his left breast. The Harmans, to a
man, wore their bullet-pouches on the left side, and with this and his arm
he so completely shielded his breast that the Indians did not fire till they
saw the old gentleman's gun nearly loaded again, when one fired on him,
and struck his elbow near the joint, cutting one of the principal arteries.
In a second more, the fearful string was heard to vibrate, and an arrow
entered Mr. Harman's breast and lodged against a rib. He had by this
time loaded the gun, and was raising it to his face to shoot one of the
Indians, when the stream of blood from the wounded artery flew into the
pan, and so soiled his gun that it was impossible to make it fire. Raising
the gun, however, had the effect to drive back the Indians, who retreated
to where the others stood with their guns empty.

"Matthias, who had remained an almost inactive spectator, now asked
permission to fire, which the old man granted. The Indian at whom he
fired appeared to be the chief, and was standing under a large beech tree.
At the report of the rifle, the Indian fell, throwing his tomahawk high
among the limbs of the tree under which he stood.

"Seeing two of their number lying dead upon the ground, and two more
badly wounded, they immediately made off, passing by Draper, who had
left his horse, and concealed himself behind a log.

"As soon as the Indians retreated, the old man fell back on the ground
exhausted and fainting from loss of blood. The wounded arm being tied
up and his face washed in cold water, soon restored him. The first words
he uttered were: 'We are whipped; give me my pipe.' This was furnished
him, and he took a whiff, while the boys scalped one of the Indians.

"When Draper saw the Indians pass him, he stealthily crept from his
hiding-place, and pushed on for the settlement, where he reported the whole
party murdered. The people assembled and started soon the following
morning to bury them; but they had not gone far before they met Mr.
Harman and his sons, in too good condition to need burying.

"Upon the tree under which the chief was killed, is roughly carved an
Indian bow, and a gun, in commemoration of the fight. The arrows which
were shot into Mr. Harman are in possession of some of his descendants."

time. It was also learned that the party was on the trail from the villages beyond the Ohio to the Cherokee towns on the Little Tennessee, and that they had come upon the camp of the hunters by chance. It was not a war party but a roving band such as might be encountered at any time in those days in the wilderness.[10]

Mrs. Wiley, upon her return, gave a good description of the Indians. She supposed the Cherokee chief to have been more than fifty years of age, possibly sixty. He was a large man, stern and hard of countenance, resourceful, full of energy and quick of mind and body for an Indian, much more cruel than his companions, and treacherous but bold and relentless. His ears and nose were decorated with Indian ornaments, among them silver rings of elaborate workmanship, some of them as much as three inches in diameter. He wore buckskin leggins and beaded moccasins, a shirt of red cloth, carried a knife and a tomahawk in his belt, had the shot-pouch and powder-horn of the white man slung over his left shoulder and under his right arm, and was armed with a long rifle which he carried muzzle forward on his shoulder. He was fierce and irascible, and Mrs. Wiley stood in much fear of him from the first. He had carried away a white woman from some Kanawha settlement a few years previous to this raid. Many years afterwards it was believed this was a Mrs. Tacket, descendants of whom live now in Johnson County, Kentucky.

Among the Shawnees of the band there was a chief. He was an old man and while a warrior he was also a sort of medicine man or priest. He was of grave and solemn mien, and like the Cherokee, had his nose and ears decorated with Indian gewgaws, but these he seldom wore while

---

10 The number of Indians belonging to the different tribes represented in the band Mr. Wiley had from his mother. This party was not on the warpath. The Indians were going to visit in the Cherokee country. Their meeting with these hunters was purely accidental.

The Settlers on their way to build the Blockhouse and establish Harman's Station

on the war-path, they being a part of his ceremonial regalia. He had a number of small silver brooches strung together in chains with which he ornamented himself, and he carried rings and other ornaments for his arms, wrists, and ankles. He worshiped the New Moon, or performed some manner of incantation at the appearance of every new moon. His songs were long and always recited with solemn dignity, often sung while he marched about a fire kindled for the purpose and upon which he flung some substance with which tobacco had been previously mixed. Age had not impaired his strength, although he was long since done with much of the ardor which had animated his youth. He was of a more kindly disposition than the other Indians. He did not make such show of his ornaments as did the Cherokee chief who carried a buckskin bag containing his silver ornaments, and another also which contained ornaments of shell, bone, brass, and copper. Mrs. Wiley gave good descriptions of the other Indians, but it is not necessary to repeat them here.

CHAPTER IV

Mrs. Wiley remembered well the state of the weather the day the attack was made upon her home. A heavy rain began at noon, and soon clouds of fog hung about the mountain tops and drifted up the valleys. The autumn frosts had turned the forests a sombre hue which showing under the dull and leaden sky aroused a sense of melancholy.

Thomas Wiley was absent from home that day. Before daylight he had set out for some trading station with a horse laden with ginseng and other marketable commodities which he would barter for domestic necessaries. Mrs. Wiley's brother, a lad of fifteen, remained with her in the absence of her husband. The trading station was a considerable distance from Wiley's residence, and it was not expected that he could reach home until late at night.

There had been born to Thomas Wiley and his wife four children, the age of the youngest being about fifteen months.

John Borders lived about two miles from the house of Wiley. Some of his sheep had broken from an enclosure and escaped into the woods. While they remained there they were in danger of destruction from wolves and other wild animals. In the morning of this day Borders had gone out to search for his sheep. He had not found them when the rain set in. After wandering awhile in the rain he found himself in the vicinity of Wiley's cabin and went down to it. He found Mrs. Wiley engaged in weaving a piece of cloth for use in her family. He called her attention to the cries and hootings of owls which could be plainly heard from different points in the woods around

the house. He said that he had heard these cries since
the rain began to fall, but had not heard them before.
While it was not unusual for the owls to call from mountain to mountain on dark and rainy days Borders was
apprehensive that the hootings heard this day came from
Indians signaling to one another. Indians always used
the cries of wild animals as such signals. Borders urged
Mrs. Wiley to take her children to his house and remain
there over night as a matter of precaution. Mr. Wiley
would pass his house on his return and could be hailed and
remain there also. Mrs. Wiley agreed to go as Borders
requested, but wished first to complete the piece of cloth,
which would require but a few minutes. As her brother
could assist her in bringing the children Borders returned
home at once through the woods and made further search
for his sheep.

To follow along the course of the creek it was a mile
from the cabin of Thomas Wiley to that of Matthias
Harman, but by the path which led over a low hill the
distance was less than half a mile. When standing in this
mountain path on the top of the range if you went down
to the south you came to Harman's house; by descending
to the north Wiley's cabin was reached.

As soon as Borders departed Mrs. Wiley made all haste
to feed and care for the domestic animals on the farm
and arrange for her absence from home over night. The
Indians were always expected in those days, but Mrs.
Wiley felt no fear. It was her judgment that no attack
would be made upon any settler until after night came on.
Usually that course would have been taken by the Indians,
but in this instance they were anxious to proceed as
rapidly as possible.

It was about four o'clock in the afternoon when Mrs.
Wiley and the children were wrapped and ready to start
to the home of Borders. Suddenly the house was filled
with Indians. They came in at the open door yelling

the war-whoop and began to strike down the children with
their tomahawks.   Little resistance could be offered by
Mrs. Wiley.   She realized the awful condition she was in,
but she tried to save her children.   She could not reach
any weapon and could only struggle to protect the little
ones.   Her brother aided her as much as he could until
he was brained with a tomahawk.   Only the youngest child
remained alive of her children and her brother.   She
caught up this child and fought off the Indians a few
moments, after which the Shawnee chief found an opportunity to seize her and claim her as his captive.   This
angered the Cherokee chief, and a controversy arose.   Mrs.
Wiley learned in some way from the actions of the two
chiefs and what they said that they supposed themselves
at the house of Matthias Harman.   She made haste to
inform them that they were not at the Harman residence
and told them her name.   It appears that there had been
some doubt as to which was Harman's house in the minds
of the savages.   For the time being Mrs. Wiley's life was
spared, also that of the child she had in her arms.   Her
slain children and her brother were scalped before her
eyes.

The Indians found that their plans had miscarried.
The family of their arch enemy had escaped, though they
had perpetrated a bloody deed in the settlement.   The
Cherokee insisted that Mrs. Wiley and her child should
be killed at once and a descent made upon Harman's house.
The Shawnee chief believed that the hunters would return
that day and that they would meet with resistance at the
Harman cabin.   It was his opinion that they should make
their escape from the settlements and continue their journey, for pursuit was certain.   The Cherokee was equally
certain that they would be followed by the settlers and
was finally brought to the opinion of the Shawnee, but he
pointed out that they could not escape if they carried any
prisoners.   The Shawnee chief contended for his right to

The Indians taking Mrs. Wiley into the Wilderness after the murder of her children and the destruction of her home

take a captive and carry her to his town. It was finally decided that the Shawnee might retain his captive for the time being, though it necessitated, as they believed, a return to the Indian towns beyond the Ohio. Their decision to follow this course saved Mrs. Wiley's life. She did not know what the Indians were saying, and only came to know what had passed long afterwards when she understood the Shawnee language. Both chiefs could speak English a little, but this discussion had been carried on in the Indian tongue. The Shawnee chief informed her that he had saved her life that she might take the place of his daughter who had recently died, the last of his children.[11]

The Indians set the house on fire, but such torrents of rain were falling that it did not completely burn. They entered the woods at a point near the house. Darkness was coming rapidly on. Mists and the black clouds of night swallowed up the valley and shut out the view. Mrs. Wiley's dog came hesitatingly after them and was permitted to follow her. They ascended a hill north of the

---

[11] In all his recitals to me Mr. Wiley never omitted to include the fact that his mother was to be the daughter of the Shawnee chief. The formal adoption, he insisted, could not be made until the Indians reached the towns of the Shawnees, consequently she could not be given in marriage to any one before they reached there. Being, to all intents and purposes, the daughter of the chief, Mr. Wiley maintained that his mother was safe from violation and escaped that humiliation. I have heard statements to the effect that an Indian daughter was born to Mrs. Wiley after her escape and return to the Virginia settlements. Mr. Burris writes me that he has heard the same thing. I have been told that Adam P. Wiley was the son of the Shawnee. That was certainly untrue, for Mr. Wiley was born in 1798. Some versions of the captivity of Mrs. Wiley had it that she was carried to Old Chillicothe and that her sale to the Cherokee occurred there, after which she was carried to the old Indian town at the mouth of Little Mudlick Creek by the Cherokee as his wife.

There was never any uniformity in these versions, and they always appeared to me as mere conjecture of those having indefinite information. It was natural, of course, for Mr. Wiley to believe that his mother escaped violation. It is the province of the historian to state all the facts in his possession, and I have performed that duty to accuracy in historical accounts in this instance.

house, marching in Indian file headed by the Cherokee chief, the Shawnee chief being hindmost with Mrs. Wiley, her child in her arms, just in front of him.

CHAPTER V

After leaving Wiley's house the Indians took a general course leading to the head of Walker's Creek. They followed mountain ways and short cuts from one valley to another, coming to Brushy Mountain, which they crossed to the head waters of Wolf Creek. When the night was far advanced they halted in a large rockhouse [12] in the range between Wolf Creek and the Bluestone River. There they made a fire under the overhanging rock and broiled some venison which a Cherokee took from a pack he carried by thongs on his back. They made a hasty meal of this venison, which appeared to refresh them all, and when the rain ceased they again set forward after extinguishing the fire and concealing as far as possible all traces of its existence. It was still quite dark. The dull dawn found them on the head waters of the Bluestone, branches of which river they waded as they came to them, though all were running high from the recent rains. They crossed the Great Flat Top Mountain and ascended the south end of one of those ridges lying in the watershed between Guyandotte and Tug rivers. This rough range extends almost to the Ohio. The great Indian trail up the Tug

---

[12] The term "rockhouse" is heard only in the South, and principally in the region of the Alleghanies south of Pennsylvania. It is not used in connection with a cave. It does not apply to a cave; a cave is entirely distinct from a rockhouse. A rockhouse is the open space beneath an overhanging rock or cliff. Rockhouses are sometimes of large extent. I have known them to be used as stables for horses and cattle. They are the favorite resorts of sheep in summer. They are cool and pleasant in the warmest weather, but having a large opening along the entire front they are poor protection from cold in winter. They are found only where the prevailing rocks are sandstone.

River often followed along its tortuous and uneven crest and from that cause it was long known as Indian Ridge, especially in its southern reaches.

The Indians made no halt during this day's travel until late in the afternoon, when, believing themselves beyond any immediate danger of being overtaken by the whites, they made a camp in a rockhouse in the head of a creek below the crest of the mountain. They had not killed any game during the day, although both bear and deer were in sight more than once. Their meal consisted of venison from the pack of the Cherokee. This venison was dried until hard, but the Indians held it in the flames of their camp fire until it was cooked a little, then they ate it. Mrs. Wiley ate some of it, also some parched corn from the wallet of one of the Indians. She was exhausted with the long and rough march of twenty-four hours she had been forced to make. She had climbed mountains and waded streams; she had forced her way through thickets of laurel and ivy, and had tramped through quagmires and over stones; she had been compelled to ascend almost perpendicular cliffs and to descend sheer precipices. Much of the time she had been drenched to the skin. Her child was in great distress and had cried until it could cry no more because of hoarseness. At this camp she saw the warriors make hoops of green boughs and over them stretch the scalps of her brother and her children. In after life she often declared that at no other time did despair so take hold of her as it did this second night of her captivity.

When the Indians lay down to sleep they bound Mrs. Wiley with strips of raw deer skin. She was in a state of nervous delirium and could not sleep, neither could she rest. Every time she closed her eyes she seemed to behold the slaughter of her children anew, and more than once she shrieked aloud. Her cries aroused the old Shawnee, who finally unbound her. He lighted a torch and carried it into the woods, returning soon with some

Mrs. Wiley trying to escape from the Indians with her child

leaves from which he made an infusion in a small vessel
he carried. He gave her some of this preparation to
drink, after which she fell into a troubled sleep that continued through the night.

The Shawnee chief aroused Mrs. Wiley before the dawn.
The Indians were preparing to depart. She was given
some corn and venison for the morning meal, and the whole
party again set forward. The mountain streams were
running bank full from the recent heavy rain, and the
Indians avoided them as much as possible by keeping to
the paths which followed the ridges. It was with much
difficulty that Mrs. Wiley could proceed. She was urged
by the Indians to quicken her pace, but her progress was
slow and painful. The only thing which enabled her to
drag herself along was the fear that if she failed to keep
up with the Indians they would kill her child. More than
once was this proposed by the Cherokee chief, and it was
acquiesced in by all the band save the old Shawnee. As
the day advanced the reserve forces of her strong constitution came to her aid and she made better time, but her
marching was not satisfactory to the Indians.

When the Indians were starting out this morning they
sent two of their number back over the trail to keep watch
for the whites, for they were confident that the hunters
would follow them. Some of the younger members of the
band believed the heavy rains had washed out their trail,
but the Cherokee said such was not the case, especially if
they should be followed by Matthias Harman. This was
one of his strong arguments in favor of killing Mrs.
Wiley's child. It was with difficulty that the old Shawnee
withstood the demands of the Cherokee chief.

At the end of this day's march an encampment was made
in a location much like that of the preceding night. The
Indians halted before the sun was down because one of
their number had killed a fat bear at the time, and they
feasted most of the night. Though the march had been

severe the distance passed had been much less than was
covered during the same time of the day before, and Mrs.
Wiley's condition had improved somewhat, but her feet
were terribly bruised and blistered. She had little hope
that her child would live through the night. There being
nothing better at hand she rubbed it well with bear's
grease, and at the suggestion of the Shawnee chief she
forced it to swallow some of the melted fat. This seemed
in a measure effective, for the morning showed improvement in the child's health. The Shawnee chief made a
decoction of some leaves boiled with the inner layers of
the bark of the white oak, which he caused Mrs. Wiley to
apply to her feet, and which gave her immediate relief.
An additional application in the morning caused still
further improvement, and this, together with the improved
condition of her child, caused Mrs. Wiley to begin the day
with more hope than she began the previous one. The
party left the camp before it was light and continued the
journey in the direction of the Ohio. A heavy rain had
fallen in the night, and it rained most of the day. A terri-
fic storm of wind and rain drove the party under a cliff
shortly before darkness came on, and they built a fire and
camped there. That camp was in the hills just west of
the head of Twelve Pole Creek. The Indian scouts who
had been sent back each day reported late at night, and
here they said they had seen no pursuers on their trail.

The Indians left their camp, as was their custom, on the
following morning before it was light. Insufficient food
and the continuous marching was rapidly exhausting Mrs.
Wiley, and she found herself unable to move forward so
rapidly as on the previous day. She was failing under
hardships and the burden of her child. The Shawnee
chief warned her of the consequences of failing to keep up
with the warriors. But try as she might she could not
satisfy her captors.

The Indians who had been sent back as scouts this

morning returned late in the day and reported that they had seen a large party of white men on horseback following their trail. This was not unexpected intelligence, but the Indians discussed earnestly what it was best to do in the matter. Some proposed an ambush of the white men, but this was not taken as the best course to follow. The Cherokee chief proposed the immediate death of the child and a change of course. Mrs. Wiley promised to keep up with the march, and with the aid of the Shawnee chief saved the life of the child for a time. The Indians turned west and descended the hills toward Tug River. They sought a small stream and waded down it until it became too deep for that purpose, when they changed to another. Mrs. Wiley kept well up for a few miles, then began to fail. Despite her utmost exertions she could not march at the rate the Indians were then going. She fell behind the Indians marching in front of her, and began to feel that her child was in great danger. She suspected that her friends were near, although the Indians had told her nothing. At length the Cherokee chief stopped. He was leading the march, and he and most of the party were far in advance. Mrs. Wiley knew what he would do when he came back to her place in the line. His arrival there meant death for her child and possibly death for herself. The Shawnee chief was following her in the water. Mrs. Wiley ran out of the stream and with her last strength ran back up its course with her child.[13] She had no partic-

[13] This stream flows into Tug River. It is the first stream of any considerable size on the West Virginia side below Marrowbone Creek. The Indians waded down the last named creek until it got too deep to allow rapid traveling; then they crossed the mountain to the creek upon which Mrs. Wiley's child was killed. Ever since the country has been settled this creek has been called Jennie's Creek, in honor of Mrs. Wiley. After she moved to Kentucky Mrs. Wiley went to this creek and identified the place where her child was killed; she identified the big beech tree against which the Cherokee chief dashed out its brains. This tree was preserved, and it was standing twenty years ago, since which time I have not heard anything concerning it.

ular object in doing this except to carry her child out of danger, and that was a vain effort. The old Shawnee was surprised, but he ran after her and caught her just as the Cherokee chief came up. She was surrounded by the Indians. The Cherokee chief seized her child by the feet and dashed out its brains against a big beech tree. He scalped it, and she was pushed back into the stream and forced to continue her flight.

It was almost dark when the party reached the Tug River, which they found much swollen from the recent rains. As the Indians arrived on its banks a violent thunder storm broke over the valley. The Indians realized that in crossing the river at once lay their only hope of escape from the party in pursuit. Their only means of crossing the stream was by swimming. With the river at the stage at which they found it that was a dangerous undertaking. At all times a swift mountain stream, it was now a raging torrent covered with drift and all manner of river-rubbish. Mrs. Wiley was amazed and terrified when told she must cross the mad stream by swimming in company with the Indians. In the gathering gloom its contortions were visible only by the fierce flashes of lightning that burned in the heavens. It seemed impossible for any one to survive a conflict with this raging river. But she was seized by two Shawnees and dragged screaming into the surging flood. One swam on either side of her. They grasped her firmly by her arms and swam easily and swiftly. They went with the current of the stream and avoided the drift with the dexterity of otters. Their position was almost upright with much of the body above the water; and they pushed but slightly against the current but were all the time working themselves toward the opposite shore. After being carried down the river what seemed to Mrs. Wiley several miles they were all cast to the west bank and found themselves in "dead" water in the mouth of a small creek. There it was much more

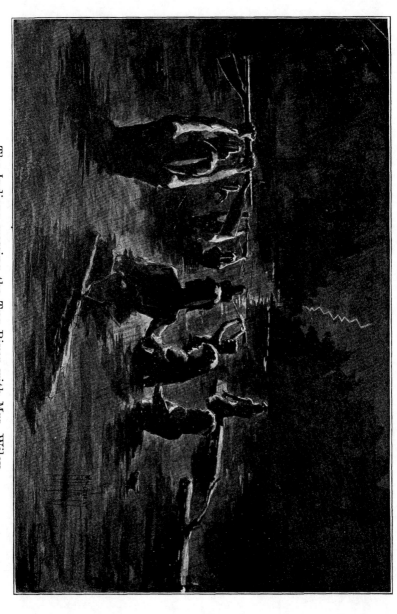

The Indians crossing the Tug River with Mrs. Wiley

difficult to swim and support the captive above the water, but they succeeded in effecting a landing. The whole party was exhausted and some time was spent in resting, after which the journey was continued. The Indians waded up the stream into the mouth of which they had been cast by the river. It led up into a very rough mountain covered with bristling thickets of laurel and ivy. The storm cleared and the air became chill as they descended the mountain range they were crossing. A large rockhouse was sought at the base of the range and a small fire made in it and the blaze screened. The Indians left this camp at dawn, and in the afternoon reached the Louisa River. There they cooked and ate a small deer which had been killed on the march and which made an insufficient meal for the party. The Louisa River was found full to the brim. After resting until almost dark the Indians crossed it as they had crossed the Tug. They went into camp under a cliff behind a mountain and built a roaring fire about which all slept through the night. In the early light of the following morning they sent out two of their number to hunt. In a short time the hunters returned with part of a buffalo they had killed in a canebrake. The day was spent in eating and sleeping. The Indians believed they had made a complete escape from their pursuers and did not again give that subject any serious consideration. As the sun was nearing the tops of the hills in the western range the party set forward again. They followed a trail which led through valleys and over rough hills, but they marched in a leisurely way. It was well for Mrs. Wiley that they made no forced marches for she was by this time worn out. The loitering marches brought the Indians to the Ohio River on the ninth day of Mrs. Wiley's captivity.

CHAPTER VI

The Indians did not descend directly to the Ohio, but came down the hills west of the Big Sandy and followed that stream about a mile to its mouth. They found an immense flood in the Ohio, something they said was unusual for that season of the year. This flood increased the difficulty of their retreat. Notwithstanding this fact, however, the Indians appeared much pleased to reach the Ohio. The younger members of the band exclaimed "O-hi-yo! O-hi-yo! O-hi-yo!" seemingly in great delight.

How to cross the Ohio was now the question for the Indians. They discussed the matter for some time without arriving at a satisfactory conclusion and finally returned to the hills to avoid the backwater, pushed far up the small streams, and kept down the Ohio. Much of the time they were not in sight of the Ohio. They reached the mouth of the Little Sandy River without finding any means to cross the Ohio and again held council to determine upon a course. They were assisted in a decision apparently by the return of two Indians whom they had sent back from the crossing of the Louisa River to spy upon the movements of the pursuing party. Their report was delivered out of the hearing of Mrs. Wiley who was beginning to understand a few words of the different Indian tongues. After several hours spent in talk the party divided. The Cherokee chief, the Cherokee warrior, two Wyandots, and two Delawares swam across the Little Sandy River and disappeared in the woods.

The remaining Indians, with Mrs. Wiley, took their way up the Little Sandy. They appeared to be in no

Mrs. Wiley rescuing her child from the Indian Ordeal in the Cherokee
Fork of Big Blaine Creek

hurry. They left the main stream at the mouth of the Dry Fork, which they followed to the head of one of its branches. They crossed the divide through the Cherokee Gap to the Cherokee Fork of Big Blaine Creek. As they were descending this creek Mrs. Wiley became seriously ill, but she concealed her condition from the Indians as long as possible, fearing she might be killed should they discover the truth. It soon became impossible for her to proceed, however, and the Indians went into camp near the mouth of the creek. They placed Mrs. Wiley in a small rockhouse near the camp and left her alone. There a son was born to her. The birth was premature and she was near death for some time, but she finally recovered and the child lived. She attributed her recovery to a season of fine weather which came on. The Indians brought her meat from the game they killed and from the first of her illness kept her a fire; but as soon as she could walk they left her to gather her own fire-wood. Knowing that it was impossible for her to escape the Indians paid little attention to her.

The Indian party spent the winter in camp at the mouth of Cherokee Creek and allowed Mrs. Wiley to live alone in the rockhouse with her child. She lost all account of time. She did not know the day of the week from the time they went into camp there until she made her escape. The Shawnee chief gave her child a name. The sojourn at this place was uneventful but for one instance. One day when the weather was becoming warmer the Shawnee chief came to the rockhouse and said the child was "three moons," meaning that its age was then about three montl s. He informed her that he was making preparations to give it the first test a boy was expected to undergo. He made no explanation and soon left the rockhouse. He returned in a short time and commanded her to take the child and follow him. He led her to the creek where the other Indians were assembled. The chief tied the child to a large slab of dry bark and set it adrift in the swift water of a small shoal. The child began to cry as soon as it felt the cold water, and this action seemed to condemn it in the minds of the warriors. They brandished their tomahawks, and Mrs. Wiley rushed into the water and rescued the infant, immediately returning to the rockhouse with it. The Indians followed her, and when they arrived at the rockhouse the Wyandot killed the child with his tomahawk and immediately proceeded to scalp it. She was not molested, but she saw that the Indians were very angry. She was permitted to bury the child in a corner of the rockhouse.

Soon after the murder of her child and while the streams were full from melting snow the Indians left their camp at the mouth of Cherokee Creek. Mrs. Wiley was not strong but was forced to keep up with the party. They followed a trail which led up Hood's Fork of Big Blaine Creek. Crossing through a gap at the head of one of its branches they came to the Laurel Fork, which they followed to that fine rolling country now known as Flat Gap, in Johnson County. From that point they followed a small stream to the main branch of Big Mudlick Creek, which they descended to the great buffalo lick from which the stream derived its name. They camped at the lick in hope of killing some game, but none came during their stay. They broke camp one morning at dawn and went down the creek, arriving during the day at an old Indian town at the mouth of Little Mudlick Creek. The actions of the Indians there made Mrs. Wiley suppose that the end of their journey had been reached and that they would remain for some time. As that is a somewhat remarkable location and the Indians kept Mrs. Wiley there until the following October a description of some of its most prominent features will not be out of place here.

Little Mudlick Creek is about three miles in length. In dry summers there are times when little water can be

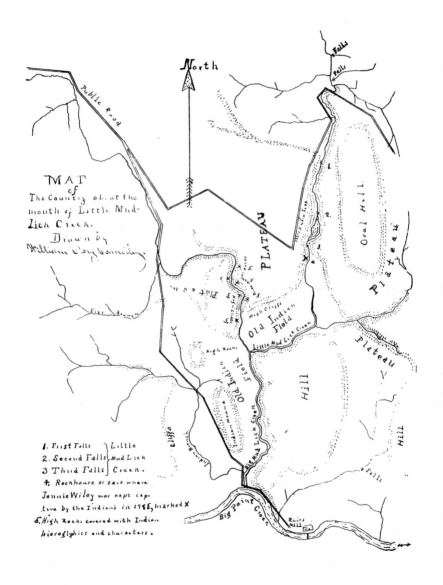

North

Public Road

MAP
of
The Country about the
mouth of Little Mud-
Lick Creek.
Drawn by
William Clay Connelley.

PLATEAU

Plateau

Plateau

Oval Hill

Plateau

Plateau

Old Indian Field

High Rocks

Little Mud Lick Creek

Hill

Hill

Old Indian Field

Cliffs

Indian Branch

Little Mud Lick Creek

Falls

Falls

Falls

Falls

1. First Falls ⎫ Little
2. Second Falls ⎬ Mud Lick
3. Third Falls ⎭ Creek.
4. Rockhouse or cave where
Jennie Wiley was kept cap-
tive by the Indians in 1788, marked X
5. High Rocks covered with Indian
hieroglyphics and characters.

Big Paint Creek

Ruins Mill

found in its bed. Its general course is from north south, but it falls into Big Mudlick Creek from the east. It joins the larger stream about half a mile from where Big Mudlick and Big Paint Creek unite. A short distance above the junction of the Mudlick creeks each stream flows through narrows or gorges formed by their having broken through a range of low hills and cut deep channels in ledges of sandstone. In the space enclosed between the two streams there is a perfectly level tract, a miniature table-land or plateau, which runs from near their junction back several hundred feet to a succession of low hills. The beds of the streams are as much as two hundred feet below this plateau, the edges of which are perpendicular and overhang the creeks. These overhanging cliffs contain caves and fissures or rockhouses and projecting ledges of sandstone to which it is difficult to gain access. At some points the rock is steep and bare from the surface of the water to its utmost height. In other places great masses of sandstone are broken from the main ledges and lie piled about the base of the cliffs in great confusion. The broader ledges, huge crevices, and long interstices in these cliffs are thickly grown with laurel and ivy, shrubs indigenous to the sandstone hills and cliffs of the South. At the base and far up the sides of the cliffs at points where sufficient footing exists grow huge hemlocks, gnarled chestnuts, and misshapen black pines, many of these overhanging the creeks. Interspersed with these are holly-trees covered in winter with scarlet berries. Along the creeks are willows and sycamore trees and sometimes slender birches. The creek bottoms were formerly covered with beech trees which long since fell before the axe of the backwoodsman. The steep ravines are choked with thickets. The plateau itself is covered with a thin and straggling growth of stunted trees and indigenous shrubs.

On the face of the cliff overhanging the waters of the larger creek were formerly found many Indian hieroglyph-

51

pictures. These pictures were usually 's of animals native to the country, such ...r, deer, panther, wolf, turkey, and a few ...es and rattlesnakes. These figures were put on the cliffs with black or red paint; no other colors were used. There was no mixing of colors; there were red groups and black groups, but nowhere were the two colors found in the same group. In no instance were the figures cut or scratched into the rock. Time, thoughtless and mischievous vandalism, and the weather have destroyed them all. In 1850, it is said, some of the groups were faintly visible, and as late as 1880 one group of deer in black, on the cliff over the larger creek, was yet very distinct.[14]

---

[14] When Johnson County, Kentucky, was first settled there were found along the Indian trail from the mouth of Mudlick Creek to the mouth of Big Paint Creek occasional trees which had been stripped of their bark from the ground to a considerable height, sometimes as far up as thirty feet. Often a tree had the bark stripped from but one side, which made a dry hard surface on that side of the tree, while the other side still lived and preserved the tree. Trees thus treated were found all along the trail, but at some points there would be found groups of them all of which had been so denuded. The smooth surface thus provided was covered by the Indians with outline figures of animals and birds, put on with a tenacious and lasting paint of two colors only — black and red. As it is not known that trees thus treated and marked were found at any other place in the United States this circumstance may be regarded as very remarkable. The signification of these paintings was never discovered, and it is not known whether they were made by but one tribe or by all the tribes inhabiting the Ohio Valley. Trees so marked were to be found all along the valley of the Big Sandy, including both branches, but so far as I could ever discover no locality had them in so great abundance as the country around the lower course of Big Paint Creek. Whether the custom had prevailed among the tribes for ages, or whether it was of recent date and origin was never known. It is known that the Shawnees, Delawares, Wyandots, Toteros, Cherokees, and Iroquois, regarded the Big Sandy Valley with peculiar and lasting veneration. They clung to it with tenacity, and it was the last stream in Kentucky to be surrendered by them. It was a favorite valley of the Mound Builders, as evidenced by many remains of their occupation.

Big Paint Creek is a large and rapid stream. Just below the town of Paintsville it flows over an inclined sandstone bed. This point has various local names, such as the "flat rock," "flat rock ford," etc. The incline is sharp, and the water in passing over it was carried with force sufficient

Beyond each of the creeks the plateau is irregularly continued. To the east across the smaller creek there is a mound-like hill the base of which rests upon an expanse of country of the same elevation as the plateau. To the north between the smaller stream and Big Paint Creek stand two such hills with bases resting upon a similar elevation. To the west beyond the larger creek the continuation of the plateau is narrow, a ledge of sandstone with its east and south sides almost perpendicular. At a little distance south of this ledge and entirely detached from it is a large mass of sandstone with sides nearly perpendicular. This rock rises from the low-lying creek bottom and has a flat top of considerable area which can be reached with difficulty. From this elevation to the mouth of Big

to excavate in the bed of the creek below it a very deep pool and to cut away the banks, giving the expansion the appearance of a lake through which the creek ran. In early times the pool was spoken of as bottomless, so great was its depth, and it was always spoken of in my time as " the deep hole." The principal boat yards of the Big Sandy Valley were around this remarkable pool; hundreds of barges for carrying tan bark, hoop poles, staves, sawed lumber, and other products of that country were built upon its banks.

Upon the south bank of the creek against the " flat rock ford " is a low cliff, beneath which there is a small rockhouse which would afford shelter for fifty or sixty people. This locality seemed to hold a fascination for the Indians. On the top of the cliff a great elm had been stripped of its bark to a height of thirty feet or more. Winding about the tree and encircling all the smooth surface made by taking off the bark was a huge rattlesnake put on with black paint. Many other trees in the vicinity were stripped or partly stripped of their bark, and painted, various animals of the country being represented. One tree in the upper end of the creek bottom in which is situated the town of Paintsville, on the spot where Rev. Henry Dickson (Dixon, it is now written by his descendants) built a grist mill to be operated by horse, mule, or ox power, and called by the early settlers a " horse mill," was painted; it was a giant elm, and it bore a huge bear put on with red paint.

There were many salt springs or " licks " in the vicinity of where Paintsville was located. Several of them were at the foot of the hills back of the town and are now covered by the washings from the cleared hillsides above them. The trees about these licks were painted by the Indians, the characters being of the same nature as those already described. From this cause the first hunters and explorers of the country called these licks " painted licks," and they named the stream upon which they were found

Mudlick Creek it is half a mile, and the land is a bottom
lying just above overflow.   This creek bottom is an old
Indian field.   At the time of the coming of the white man
it contained many mounds.   There is one very large mound
or mound-shaped hill covered with broken sandstone.
Human bones, stone axes, spear and arrow heads of flint,

Paint Lick Creek, and it is so marked on the map of Kentucky in the
1797 edition of Imlay's America. The name was given by Matthias Harman and his associates. When Colonel John Preston, Judge French, and
others of Virginia who speculated in the lands of the Louisa River Valley,
wished to name the trading station which they established on the present
site of Paintsville in 1790, they called it Paint Lick. The Rev. Henry
Dickson came from North Carolina and bought the land about the old
station and laid out the present town and named it Paintsville. Prestonsburg was also founded by Col. Preston and others, and first called Preston's
Station. The station was established in 1799. After Vancouver left the
forks of the Big Sandy a town was established there and named Balclutha.
On the Imlay map already mentioned Paint Lick and Balclutha are both
marked. To Johnson County belongs the honor of having within her bounds
the sites of both the first and second settlements made in the Big Sandy
Valley and in Eastern Kentucky.

Above the mouth of Big Paint Creek there is a river bottom extending
up the Louisa River about a mile. At a point near the creek bank, and at
an equal distance from the river, there is a large mound, the work of pre-
historic inhabitants of the valley. Several hundred feet up the river, and
directly south of this mound, there is another, not quite so large. At an
equal distance south of this second mound there is a third one a little
smaller than the second. And there is at an equal distance south from
this third mound a fourth one still a little smaller than the third. There
is a mound just back of the rockhouse overlooking the flat rock ford. These
mounds were covered with large trees when first seen by white men. The
original public highway up the Big Sandy River was laid out to cut the
north side of the second mound. In making this public road the mound
was cut, and the skeleton of a man of large size was found. It was enclosed in a sort of rude box made by placing flat thin river stones about
and over it. It was on the land of Valentine Van Hoose, and I saw one of
his sons wantonly destroy the skull of this skeleton. The large mound was
opened a few years since, and the skeleton of a man was found, or rather
the plain imprint of one, but the bones had perished. These mounds were
made of layers of different kinds of earth, and there were several layers
of clean river sand in them. Layers of ashes and charcoal were found, in-
dicating that it may have been the custom of the builders to burn their
dead there, or place the ashes of their dead there after the bodies had been
burned at some other place. The Cherokee Indians said to the early settlers there, in speaking of these mounds: "There is fire in all those
mounds." What they meant by this statement they could not explain.

The Falls of Little Mudlick Creek in Winter

[*Photograph by Luther, Louisa, Ky.*]

carved shells, and stone pipes were here turned up in great abundance by the plows of the first settlers.

The diminutive gorge of Little Mudlick Creek is a thing of wild and romantic beauty. The first fall is but ten feet. One hundred feet below is a fall of about six feet, below

---

Many pipes, arrowheads, spearheads, and stone axes were found in and about these mounds. The best specimen of the stone axe I ever saw was found there by my nephew and is now in my collection.

To the southwest of Paintsville and in plain view of the town there is a solid sandstone ledge rising from the top of a hill to a height far above the surrounding forest. This immense mass of sandstone is locally known as the "hanging rock." On the hilltop back of this great cliff there are a number of Indian graves covered with a great quantity of loose sandstone fragments which have evidently been carried there from a considerable distance. Indian graves of this description are very common in Eastern Kentucky, and they are always found on the tops of ridges. I never saw any account of such graves in any work on the Mound Builders.

Above the small cliff at the "flat rock ford" the first explorers found a number of decaying cabins. The Ohio Indians said that they and the French had built them many years before, and that they had lived there. They also said that the Toteros or Shatara Indians had lived there before they built the cabins. These Totero Indians had a town on the Lick Fork of Jennie's Creek, extending from the forks of that stream to the point now known as Hager Hill. The Shawnees and Cherokees pointed out to the early settlers the sites of many towns occupied by the Totero Indians. I shall locate them in some future work.

It is a tradition in our family that some of the Connellys, probably Harmon Connelly and his brother Thomas, Daniel Boone, Matthias Harman, Walter Mankins, and a number of other parties, among them James Skaggs and Henry Skaggs, descended the Louisa River about 1763 in search of a suitable place to settle. They camped about these old cabins at the mouth of Big Paint Creek for six weeks. The river and creek bottoms were covered with a rank growth of cane, much of it so high that it would conceal a man on horseback. The fierceness of the Indians made it impossible for them to locate there then. They killed much game. Great herds of buffalo roamed the country at the time. John Howe, Esq , the famous millwright, son-in-law of Rev. Henry Dickson, has often told me of this journey of the Connellys, Boone, and others. He also said that the river was sometimes so full of buffalo wallowing in the shoals that it was impossible to get a canoe either up or down until the shaggy animals had departed. Mr. Howe and many other pioneers of Johnson County have often told me that Simon Kenton occupied the old cabins at the mouth of Big Paint Creek two winters, or parts of two winters, 1773-74 and 1774-75. He hunted in that region during those winters and it is very probable that the old settlers were right in saying he lived in one of these old cabins.

which the stream expands into a lakelet fringed with
mountain evergreens.   A short distance below this lakelet
the stream plunges some fifty or sixty feet into pools
overhung with the ever-present mountain evergreens.
From this point the stream has a rapid descent over shoals
of boulders and brook-stones to the larger creek.   The
gorge was heavily timbered with hemlocks, oaks, beeches,
holly-trees, laurel and ivy.

The Shawnees told Mrs. Wiley that in ancient times
their ancestors had their villages about the junction of the
Mudlick creeks, also all along Big Paint Creek from the
mouth of Big Mudlick Creek to the Big Sandy River.   They
also told her that they never passed through that part of
the country without visiting Little Mudlick Creek and the
country about their ancient village.

CHAPTER VII

The Indians holding Mrs. Wiley in captivity arrived at the mouth of Little Mudlick Creek about the first of April, possibly as much as a week or ten days earlier than that. They took up their abode in a rockhouse in the face of the cliff on the east side of the plateau. This rockhouse was just below the falls of Little Mudlick Creek, but at a higher elevation in the cliff than is the bed of the creek at the falls. The ledge at the entrance of the rockhouse overhangs the creek which runs a hundred feet or more below it, and the entrance is sixty feet at least below the top of the cliff. It is reached by following a narrow ledge along the face of the cliff from a point opposite the upper falls. This rockhouse is of considerable extent. It afforded a safe retreat for the party and one almost inaccessible to enemies if properly defended by even a few persons. It afforded a cool and pleasant habitation in summer.

The manner of life of the party was not unlike the daily life in an Indian village. Mrs. Wiley was compelled to perform all the drudgery of the camp. The warriors lounged about the caves and slept when not hunting or scouting. Hunting was not extensively engaged in, summer peltries being of poor quality. Only enough game was killed to furnish food for the party. Usually turkeys, deer, and buffalo were easily found near the camp, though the Indians often went to the great lick on Big Mudlick Creek to kill buffalo, especially when visited by other bands. They sometimes hunted on what is now known as Barnett's Creek, also on Big Paint Creek between that stream and Big Mudlick Creek. They sometimes required

Mrs. Wiley to follow them and bring in the game they
killed. She was shown how to care for the skins of the
animals killed. She gathered the wood for the camp fires.
As the Indians had no axe she was obliged to gather the
dry branches which had fallen from the trees, and before
the summer was over these were exhausted near the camp.
The French and the Indians had discovered lead in that
vicinity, and Mrs. Wiley was made to carry the ore from
the lead mines to the east edge of the plateau and there
smelt it out to be used for bullets for the guns. To do this
she had to collect a great quantity of wood and build a hot
fire which had to be maintained for some hours. When
the lead was melted from the ore it was conducted through
small trenches to the bottom of a depression which Mrs.
Wiley had made for the purpose and which was to be seen
as late as 1880. It was just above the entrance to the
rockhouse. She was also made to plant some corn in the
old Indian field which had been the site of the old Indian
town.

The Indians remained at the camp on some mysterious
mission, as Mrs. Wiley judged. They were often visited
by other bands, some of which contained as many as twenty Indians. Sometimes these visiting bands remained
several days; at other times they departed in a few hours.
Mrs. Wiley learned the Shawnee language, also something
of other Indian tongues. She made many efforts to hear
what the visiting Indians said to her captors, but was
never able to get any information of benefit to her. The
Shawnee chief told Mrs. Wiley he would take her to the
Indian towns beyond the Ohio when Indian summer came
on, at which time he expected a large force of Indians to
arrive and relieve him. Mrs. Wiley sought an opportunity
to escape after this conversation with the old Shawnee,
but none presented itself that she could believe promised
success. She was entirely ignorant of the general physical features of the country in which she was held, although

The torture of the Captive

she believed that she was nearer the Virginia settlements than when she was on the Ohio River. She had feigned sleep in the hope that her captors would say something about the settlements of white people that she might hear, but they never did so. There had been times when she was out of sight of her captors and might have escaped, but never having been able to bring herself to believe the effort would prove successful, she had waited for a more favorable opportunity. As the time approached when she was to be taken to the Indian towns she became more determined upon escape, or upon death in the effort. Her resolution in this matter was overturned by an event wholly unexpected.

One day about the end of October the Indians were aroused from their indolent loungings by the quavering war-whoop cried by some party about the mouth of Big Mudlick Creek. The Shawnee chief answered the war-cry, and it was repeated. The Shawnee chief informed his party that the Cherokee chief had been on the war-path, had lost some of his warriors, and was now coming into camp with a captive white man. War-whoops were exchanged, and guns were fired by both parties. The Shawnee chief led his party to the plateau to receive the Cherokee chief and his warriors, who soon arrived. The Cherokee chief was followed by a mongrel band of some twenty Indians, and he brought with him a white man as prisoner. Mrs. Wiley supposed this prisoner to be about twenty years old, though she was not permitted to come near enough to him to have any conversation with him. This captive was terribly beaten when he arrived on the plateau.

Mrs. Wiley was sent back to the rockhouse when the Cherokee chief had talked with the Shawnee chief. The Cherokee gave her a kettle and told her to cook him some meat as soon as she could. She built up a fire in the rockhouse and slung the kettle, which she filled with bear meat

and venison. She could hear the mad howling, whooping,
and screeching of the warriors on the height above her,
also the discharge of guns and the thumping and stamping
of feet in an Indian dance. Shortly after dark the whole
band came down from the plateau, and the captive was not
with them. It did not take her long to gather from the
conversation of the Indians that the prisoner had been
tortured at the stake. The Cherokee chief was in a great
rage, sullen and savage. He did not remain long in the
camp but returned to the heights above with his hands full
of meat from the kettle. Mrs. Wiley was rudely treated
by the Indians recently arrived, and the Shawnee chief
and his followers were excited and blood-thirsty. The
camp was overflowing with whooping Indians threatening
to kill her, and for the first time the Shawnee chief did not
stand her friend. She appealed to him but he did nothing
to quiet the howling mob, and he left the camp to join the
Cherokee. Finally the Indians left the camp and went
above, yelling along the gorge above the falls. Mrs.
Wiley was more at ease when she heard them whooping
on the plateau, but what the night would bring forth she
could not tell.[15]

An hour or two after dark a band of Indians, all of the
late arrivals, came down from the assembly. They tied

---

[15] Mr. Wiley was positive of the death of this white man. Mrs.
Wiley did not see him tortured, nor did she see his dead body. She said
the captive was tortured on the plateau overlooking Big Mudlick Creek.
The fire about which the Indians were gathered when she was taken to the
plateau was nearer the falls of Little Mudlick. Mr. Wiley and I searched
the plateau more than once for evidences of fire, and at a point near where
Mrs. Wiley believed the captive was burned we found charcoal, but of course
there was no way in which it could be connected with the death of the
captive. In many versions of the story of Mrs. Wiley there was no mention of the death of this prisoner. As his name was never known and
nothing was known about him there was little to keep the interest in his
death in the minds of the people. The older generation, though, had a distinct recollection of the burning of this young man. He came to Mrs.
Wiley in her strange dream and pointed out the settlements of the white
men.

Mrs. Wiley tied to the stake to be tortured by the Indians

Mrs. Wiley's hands with a strip of raw hide, by one end of which she was led to the height where the Indians were assembled about a big fire. The dancing ceased when she arrived. The Cherokee chief appeared as the commander of the Indians and told her that she was to be burned. She appealed to the Shawnee chief, but he made no definite answer. There was no sympathy for her in the mad band. She remembered the cruelties and many outrages she had suffered at the hands of the Indians, and as no prospect of escape came to her or seemed likely to come in the future even should she live, she was the more easily reconciled to death. In after years she affirmed that concern for her life and all earthly things departed from her, leaving her calm and collected. In this frame of mind she was bound to the tree, a small oak from which all the lower branches had been cut. Her demeanor seemed to please the Cherokee chief. Because of her courage or from some other cause which was never known to her, proceedings in the execution were suspended. The Indians retired for council and talked for a long time, as Mrs. Wiley believed. When they returned the Cherokee chief informed Mrs. Wiley that he had bought her from the Shawnee and that he would take her to his town on the Little Tennessee where she could teach his wives (he spoke as though he had quite a number of them) to write and to weave cloth like her dress. He unbound her and led her back to the camp in the rockhouse, followed by the Shawnee chief. There the fire was lighted anew. The Cherokee chief produced a buckskin bag from which he counted down to the Shawnee five hundred little silver brooches about as large as the silver dime of to-day, the price he had agreed to pay for Mrs. Wiley. They were received by the Shawnee as though he had a supreme contempt for money, and swept by him from the buckskin upon which they had been counted to him into a bag similar to that from which they had been taken. This bag he placed in his pack and lay down by the fire to sleep.

The Cherokee chief bound Mrs. Wiley with raw thongs cut from a buffalo hide, which he drew very tight, causing her great pain. He returned to the plateau and was gone a long time. He came back with several of his band some time in the night, and all slept in the rockhouse.

CHAPTER VIII

It was late in the day when John Borders returned home from the search for his sheep, and a thick and foggy darkness was settling over the valley of Walker's Creek. When he found that Mrs. Wiley had not yet arrived at his house he feared that harm had come to her and her family, and her sister, Mrs. Borders, was distressed and anxious. Borders sought a neighbor who lived near him and together they went to Wiley's house, which they found partly burned. After some time spent in a cautious examination of the place they ventured to enter the house, where they found the bodies of the slain children. The animals about the place were excited and Borders believed the Indians were yet lying in wait to do further murder. Not finding Mrs. Wiley and the young child they were uncertain of their fate, but they supposed none of the family had escaped death. No light was kindled by Borders and his companion, and after a short time spent in making the examination by which they learned the facts set out above they left the house and alarmed the settlers.

The Indians had been seen by no one, and the uncertainty in the minds of the people as to their number and further purpose spread terror in the settlement. No attempt could be made to follow the Indians during the night. Those most capable of determining just what to do in this extremity were out of the settlement and it was not known when they would return. On the following morning a number of the settlers gathered at Wiley's cabin and looked the premises over carefully, but the trail of the savages was not discovered. From some cause it was supposed that the Indians had gone down the New River. Thomas Wiley and a dozen settlers followed the Indian road down that stream hoping to come up with the Indians, but no tidings of Mrs. Wiley came from that pursuit.

In the afternoon of the day after the attack upon Wiley's house, Matthias Harman and the hunters returned to the settlement. The swollen streams and the heavy loads carried by their horses had delayed them twenty-four hours; but for these impediments they would have arrived in time to have prevented the murders committed by the Indians. The confidence of the hunters that they would arrive in the settlement before the Indians, had caused them to neglect to send a runner to warn the settlers of their danger.

Immediately upon his return Matthias Harman went to the house of Wiley where he found many of the settlers. He made a minute examination of the country around the house. In the hills north of the house he found evidences that the Indians had passed that way. He followed this discovery some miles, and upon his return to the cabin he assured the settlers that Mrs. Wiley was alive and a prisoner, that she was carrying her child which had been spared, and that the Indians would follow the Tug River war-trail and try to cross the Ohio to their towns. It was his opinion that the Cherokee chief was the leader of the band, the number of which he had determined from the trail. He was confident that he could overtake the Indians and recover the prisoners. His purpose to do this was determined upon at once.

Harman was a bold and active man. He believed this raid was made more by accident than design and that it indicated no uprising of the Indians nor any purpose to harass the settlements. It was not regarded as of sufficient importance to delay the settlement to be made at the mouth of John's Creek. He assembled those interested

Finding the Trail of the Indians who carried away Mrs. Wiley

in that enterprise and gave them instructions as to what they should carry with them, when to set out, what to do in case they should arrive before he could return there from pursuit of the Indians, and the most favorable route for them to take on the journey. There were about twenty-five men in this colony, but the exact number is not known, and their names are lost to us. We know that among them were Matthias Harman, Absalom Lusk, Henry Skaggs, James Skaggs his brother, Robert Hawes, Daniel Harman, Adam Harman, and Henry Harman. It is believed that a man named Horn, also one named Leek, were with the colonists. Harman selected ten of the most experienced Indian fighters to go with him in pursuit of the party having Mrs. Wiley and her child in captivity. Thomas Wiley was not a member of the colony and did not go out with them.[16]

Matthias Harman and his company of hunters set out early in the day in pursuit of the Indians. So confident that he was right did Harman feel that he did not at first attempt to follow the trail made by the savages, but went directly to the head waters of the Bluestone River and crossed the Great Flat Top Mountain. He found the trail of the Indians in the hills about the head of the Tug River; it followed the old Indian warpath as Harman had conjectured. This ancient way was so well defined that it required no effort to discover and follow it, which made their pursuit rapid and certain. Each camp of the Indians was discovered, and it was plain that the Indians were being gained upon every day.

If the Indians had not left the old war-path and turned down the small streams to Tug River they would have been overhauled by Harman and his party in a few hours.

---

[16] Mr. Wiley had not returned from the pursuit made down the New River, so his son always said. He also said that his father was unnerved by the destruction of his family, and that he was at the time unfit for the warpath.

It was difficult traveling on horseback along the small streams, for they were frequently choked with thickets. This caused delay when rapid movement was so necessary. Harman saw that the Indians were not far in advance and were aware of the presence of the party in pursuit. Just before night they found the body of Mrs. Wiley's child, which they buried in a shallow grave hastily dug with tomahawks and scalping knives. A few minutes after the Indians had plunged into the water and crossed Tug River Harman and his men stood upon the spot they had left. It was impossible to get the horses across the river in its flooded condition on such a night. The party camped on the bank of the river and spent the night in building rafts upon which to carry over the baggage in the morning.

Harman effected a safe crossing early the following day. It was past noon when he again found the Indian trail, which wound through a country so rough and hilly that it was well nigh impossible to follow it with horses. When he arrived at the point where the Indians had crossed the Louisa River it was the unanimous opinion of all the hunters that it was useless to follow the trail further. They all believed that it would be impossible to come up with the Indians. Mrs. Wiley was relieved of the burden of her child, and the Indians being apprised of the pursuit would hold their course to the rough, bush-grown, stony ridges where horses could scarcely go. So, with regret, the pursuit was abandoned at the Louisa River.

From the point where the Indian trail was abandoned Harman and his company ascended the Louisa River to the mouth of John's Creek and went into camp in the old hunting lodge built there by Harman more than thirty years before. There the river runs against the bluff on its west side, leaving a broad bottom on the east side of the river below the mouth of John's Creek. It was an ideal place for a pioneer settlement. The great war-path

up the river ran on the west side of the stream at that
point. There the stream is deep. John's Creek is a
stream of considerable size, having its sources in the mountain ranges about the head waters of the Tug and Louisa
rivers. Should the larger streams be beset with Indians
the valley of the smaller one would afford a safe way to
the settlements in Virginia.

The bottom in which it was designed to build the fort of
the settlement was then covered with trees ranging in size
from the shrub to the giant sycamore with its girth of
forty feet. These trees were of several varieties – birch,
beech, maple, linn, oak, poplar, and others. It was covered with a thick growth of cane which furnished winter
pastures for buffalo, elk, and deer, and which was an indi-
cation of deep and lasting fertility.

The colonists expected directly from Virginia did not
arrive for some days after the coming of Harman and his
company. Their horses were heavily packed, and their
progress through forests and over streams was necessar-
ily slow. High water hindered much.

The site selected for the fort was almost half a mile
below the mouth of John's Creek and about one hundred
yards back from the east bank of the Louisa River. The
fort was built on the plan common to the forts in frontier
settlements. It was about twenty feet square and two
stories in height. The upper story projected beyond the
walls of the lower story about two feet on every side, and
this extra space was floored with heavy timbers in which
loop-holes were cut through which to fire down upon
besieging Indians should they ever come to such close
quarters. The walls of both stories were provided with
openings through which to fire upon a foe. The door or
gate was made of split oak timbers six inches in thickness.
It was hung upon strong wooden hinges made by the
hunters, opened inward, and was secured by an immense
beam of oak. The roof sloped up from each of the four

sides of the fort to a point in the center, and was made of
thick slabs of white oak timber "pinned" to the log "ribs"
or rafters with long wooden pins or pegs driven into holes
bored with an auger. A small stream flowed from the
hills back of the bottom and passed close by the fort, and
upon it the settlers relied for water. The timber about
the fort was cut off close to the ground and burned back
the full space of rifle range. This was done to deprive
the Indians of cover should they ever besiege the fort.

This rude and strong building thus erected by the rough
backwoodsmen of the Virginia frontier, all of whom were
as brave and hardy as any who ever founded a frontier
post, was the famous blockhouse. The settlement commenced by its erection was called

HARMAN'S STATION

It was the first settlement made in Eastern Kentucky.
There was at that time no settlement in either of the
present counties of Pike, Floyd, Lawrence, Boyd, Greenup,
Carter, Elliott, Morgan, Wolfe, Magoffin, Breathitt, Knott,
Letcher, or Martin. There were no settlements on the
Tug River, and none in any of the present counties of
West Virginia touching that stream.

This fort was built by Matthias Harman and backwoodsmen whom he had induced to cast their lots with
him in the wilderness.

The fort was built in the winter of 1787-88.[17]

---

[17] In the preface it was announced that the dates fixed by Mr. Wiley
would be followed. This is the date fixed by him. I have no doubt
as to its accuracy. I refer again to the map to be found in Imlay's *American Topography*. The author says: " In order to communicate a distinct
idea of the present complexion of the State of Kentucky, I have drawn a
map from the best authorities, from which you will discern that Kentucky
is already divided into nine counties; and villages are springing up in every
part within its limts, while roads have been opened to shorten the distance
to Virginia." Harman's Station is correctly located on the said map.
The site of Vancouver's attempted settlement is marked " Vancouvers."
Relative to that attempt I set out an affidavit made by John Hanks in 1838,

Vancouver's Post at the Forks of the Big Sandy River, opposite Louisa, Kentucky, 1789

when Hanks was in his seventy-fifth year. It was first published by Dr. Ely in his work on the Big Sandy Valley:

" I was employed by Charles Vancouver in the month of February, 1789, along with several other men, to go to the forks of Big Sandy River, for the purpose of settling, clearing and improving the Vancouver tract, situated on the point formed by the junction of the Tug and Levisa Forks, and near where the town of Louisa now stands. In March, 1789, shortly after Vancouver and his men settled on said point, the Indians stole all their horses but one, which they killed. We all, about ten in number, except three or four of Vancouver's men, remained there during that year, and left the next March, except three or four men left to hold possession. But they were driven off in April, 1790, by the Indians. Vancouver went East in May, 1789, for a stock of goods, and returned in the fall of the same year. We had to go to the mouth of the Kanawha River, a distance of eighty-seven miles, for corn, and no one was settled near us; probably the nearest was a fort about thirty or forty miles away, and this was built may be early in 1790. The fort we built consisted of three cabins and some pens made of logs, like corn cribs, and reaching from one cabin to the other.

" We raised some vegetables and deadened several acres of ground, say about eighteen, on the point, but the horses being stolen, we were unable to raise a crop.   (Signed)   JOHN HANKS."

The nearest fort, "about thirty or forty miles away," which was " built may be early in 1790," was the fort erected in rebuilding the blockhouse put up by Matthias Harman and his associates in the winter of 1787-88, and which had been destroyed by the Indians, who burned it. The settlers who had been obliged to return to Virginia at the time of its destruction, returned with reinforcements in the winter of 1789-90 and built another fort in the Blockhouse Bottom. Although often attacked, they never again abandoned the settlement.

CHAPTER IX

After passing through the horrors of such an ordeal as that to which she had been subjected Mrs. Wiley found it impossible to sleep. She had nerved herself to face death with resignation, and her nerves were unstrung with the relaxation following her unexpected deliverance from the stake. And she was troubled by the change of masters. She feared the Cherokee. He was in every way different from the Shawnee chief. He was quick and energetic of action, cruel, savage, and treacherous by nature, always restless and anxious to be moving. While she believed that she owed her life to his interference in her behalf she was not sure the future would prove that she would have much to be thankful for in that matter. Her chance of escape seemed cut off and that troubled her; she regretted that she had not made the effort to escape months before. While pondering over these things she fell into a broken and troubled sleep. She found this a most strange sleep for she seemed more awake than ever. She was never sure she was asleep at all, but she always insisted that she saw this vision or had this remarkable dream: The young man so lately tortured by the Indians came to her bearing in his hand a lamp made from the bleached skull of a sheep, the brain cavity of which was filled with buffalo tallow in which was a wick that was burning brightly. The young man did not speak, but by signs indicated that she must follow him. Then her bonds fell away. The young man threaded the deep defiles of the forest with the flame of his lamp fluttering in the wind. He did not look back to see if she were following him. Arriving at a steep mountain of great height he rapidly ascended it. When he reached the top he blew strongly upon his lamp-flame which immediately leaped to a height sufficient to reveal the whole country below. She looked where he pointed across a river. There stood a fort erected by white men. As she was anxiously appealing to him for information as to who dwelt there the light paled, flickered a moment, then was gone. She was left alone in the darkness, and was immediately roused from her slumber. This dream or manifestation or phenomena, by whatever name, was repeated twice, the last time being just as the Indians began to stir in the camp.[18]

Mrs. Wiley was unbound by the Cherokee, and informed by him that it was his purpose to set out on the journey to his town in a day or two, but that he was going that morning to the great buffalo lick on Big Mudlick Creek to kill game. It was not long until the whole band of Indians left the camp. Mrs. Wiley was again bound and left in the camp in the rockhouse. She soon fell into a deep sleep from which she was wakened by the roaring of a heavy storm of wind and rain. The instant that she awoke the peculiar dream came to her mind with great force. It seemed to be a call to her to make an effort to escape; at least, she so regarded it, and she decided to act upon it. She saw the wind was blowing the rain into one corner of the rockhouse. She rolled herself over and over until she lay in this rain blown in by the wind. It was but a short time until the raw-hide thongs with which she was

[18] To those familiar with psychology and psychical phenomena remarkable dreams or manifestations to one under stress of nervous excitement or great strain or disturbance of the mental faculties are not strange; they are not impossible, improbable, nor even unusual. Volumes could be filled with authentic instances of such dreams or manifestations. Mrs. Wiley always believed she was assisted by this dream to make her escape. She believed after this dream that there were white people in the country about her. The route by which the settlement could be reached was unknown to her and had not been seen in her dream. The young man led her straight through the woods to a high mountain which does not in fact exist. But she saw it in her dream, and from the top of it she saw the fort in a settlement of her own people.

bound were soaked and became slippery and easily removed. When free she bound her dog to a large stone to
prevent his following her, seized a tomahawk and a scalping knife, and descended quickly to the bed of Little Mudlick Creek. She waded that stream to its junction with the
larger stream, which she waded to Big Paint Creek. There
she remembered that she had no well-defined plan of action, but after a little time spent in reflection she remembered that she had seen a river in her dream, and concluded
that she might reach this river by wading continuously
down stream. She acted upon that conclusion. She
found it difficult to wade in Big Paint Creek. It is a
deep, swift stream, and the heavy rain quickly raised the
small streams flowing into it, and they carried in muddy
water, which soon made it impossible for her to determine
the depth. She was often carried off her footing, and
more than once was in danger of drowning.

Big Paint Creek makes a big bend which she was compelled to follow around, and it was growing dusk when she
was at the mouth of the Rockhouse branch. At the mouth
of Jennie's Creek she crossed Paint Creek. She waded
up Jennie's Creek, which the heavy rain had put out of its
banks. Wind and rain continued all night. When she
reached the forks of Jennie's Creek she was almost exhausted, and for a time there she was much puzzled as to
which branch of the stream she should follow. Her choice
of branches was right; she turned to the left and followed
the Lick Fork. In half a mile she was again compelled
to choose between two branches of the stream, for there
the Middle Fork falls into the Lick Fork. She again turned to the left, and again her choice was right. She followed
the Lick Fork to the mouth of a small branch coming in
from the east. Here she left the larger stream and followed the little one to its head, where she crossed through
a gap to the stream now known as the Bear Branch, which
she descended to its junction with Little Paint Creek.

Continuing down the latter stream she stood upon the bank of the Louisa River as the dull dawn of a cloudy morning appeared in the east. It is unnecessary to dwell here upon the exhausted condition of Mrs. Wiley. She had waded against swift currents of overflowed streams for more than twelve hours, and had been wading for as much as eighteen hours. She dragged herself up the bank of the river and soon came opposite the blockhouse. She saw women and children there, but no man was in sight. She called out to make her presence known and for assistance to cross the river. So unexpected a cry alarmed the people at the fort, and they went in hurriedly and closed the gate.[19]

Here was a wholly unlooked-for discouragement. Mrs. Wiley was impatient and anxious, fully expecting to be followed by the savages. Seeing now the blockhouse, she reasoned that the Indians knew of its existence and would seek her in that direction. She was fearful that they might appear at any minute. She continued to call to the people in the fort, calling out her name and saying that

[19] Mrs. Wiley always insisted that she had no knowledge of the existence of the blockhouse when she left the rockhouse at the falls of Little Mudlick Creek. She had seen a fort beyond a river in her dream the night before her escape, and she supposed that by descending the creeks she would reach the river. Her contention is upheld by the facts developed in the flight. It was almost dark when she was at the mouth of the Rockhouse branch, and at the mouth of Jennie's Creek it was dark and was raining very hard. She said something told her she must cross to Jennie's Creek and follow it. To do this was to abandon her original plan of following down stream until she found the river. At the mouth of Jennie's Creek she was not two miles from the Indian camp. If she had known anything of the route up Jennie's Creek she could have reached the mouth of the creek in less than an hour by following the route of the present highway between the two points, and the amount of rain falling would have enabled her to wade small streams all the way and conceal her trail. Her ignorance of the physical features of the surrounding country saved her; for it was afterward discovered that when the Indians found that she had escaped they supposed that she had gone directly to the mouth of Jennie's Creek, and they followed that route in their first search for her. While it was yet light they were scouring the banks of Paint Creek and those of the lower courses of Jennie's Creek seeking some

she had escaped from the Indians, whom she expected to follow her. After what appeared to her to be a long time an old man came out of the fort. She recognized him at once as Henry Skaggs, an old-time friend of her father. It did not require much time for her to convince him that she was Jennie Wiley, and that she stood in great danger of being recaptured by the Indians. Skaggs knew the Cherokee chief well. He saw that no time was to be lost in getting her across the river. He told Mrs. Wiley that the men of the fort, except himself, had gone away early in the morning with the canoes. He said they would not return for some time, and that he would be compelled to construct a raft upon which to bring her over. He advised her to endeavor to swim across should the Indians appear, as it was his opinion that she would suffer death if recaptured.

A dead mulberry tree stood on the bank of the river and Skaggs and the women went vigorously to work to fell it. It was tall and had but few branches. When it fell it very fortunately broke into three pieces of about equal length. These logs were hastily rolled into the river and bound to-

---

sign of her, and finding none they abandoned the idea that she had set out for the blockhouse over that route. From the footprints of the Indians discovered by the settlers and other signs left by the Indians, they supposed that the savages had not been gone an hour when Mrs. Wiley reached the mouth of Jennie's Creek.

Jennie's Creek was given its name in her honor and because she made her escape in wading several miles against its rapid current. Mrs. Wiley said that it was perfectly plain to her that she must take the left-hand branch, as she was traveling, at the forks of Jennie's Creek. And the same thing occurred at the mouth of the Middle Fork. And it would seem a miracle that any one could find the mouth of the small branch where she turned out of the Lick Fork. It must be remembered that it was pitch dark, and that the whole country was covered with a heavy forest, beneath the boughs of which it would be dark on even a starlight night. The darkness, dense as it was, had torrents of rain to augment it. The streams were running bank full, and for many miles she pushed against the current. Considered from any point, the achievements of Mrs. Wiley that night were most remarkable. I doubt if it is equaled in all the annals of the Border. Her adventures have in them all the requisites for a romance of border life, and the subject is worthy the ablest pen.

Mrs. Wiley and Henry Skaggs crossing the River on a Raft

gether with long grapevines pulled down from the forest trees where they grew wild. Placing two rifles upon the raft Skaggs pushed out into the river which was full to overflow, and which was carrying much drift. After being carried far down the stream Skaggs made a landing. Mrs. Wiley stepped upon the rude raft and it was again pushed into the stream. When in mid-stream the raft was caught by drift and nearly pulled to pieces but by hard work both raft and drift were brought to some overhanging trees standing on the east bank. The branches of these trees were seized and the raft brought to shore about half a mile below the blockhouse.

When Mrs. Wiley and Skaggs had gone up the river to the fort and were about to enter the gate Indian yells broke from the thickets over the Louisa. A moment later a large band of Indians came into view, among them the Cherokee chief; and with them was Mrs. Wiley's dog. The Cherokee chief saw Mrs. Wiley at the entrance to the fort. He called out to her to know why she had left him after he had saved her life and paid his silver for her. He insisted that she had not treated him as she should have done, and closed his appeal with the words, "honor, Jennie, honor!" She did not reply to him. Skaggs fired his rifle in the direction of the savages, though the distance was too great for the range of small arms. At the discharge of the rifle the Cherokee turned about, and with a defiant gesture [20] uttered a fearful whoop, in which he was joined by his warriors. Seeing that Mrs. Wiley had escaped and that he could not recapture her, the Cherokee chief disappeared in the woods, followed by his savage companions and Mrs. Wiley's dog.

The report of the gun discharged by Henry Skaggs brought the men back to the blockhouse. Later in the day, after some preparation, the men crossed the river and followed the trail of the Indians almost to Little Mudlick

[20] Patted his buttocks.

Creek. From Mrs. Wiley's account of the number of Indians at the camp the hunters believed they had a force too small to attack them, so they returned after having gone to the mouth of Jennie's Creek. It was not improbable that the Indians would attack the fort soon, and upon the return of the hunters things were put in a posture of defense. No attack was made upon the blockhouse, but the Indians prowled about it for several days, and they were in the vicinity for some weeks.

Mrs. Wiley found friends in the blockhouse. Most of the settlers were well known to her in Virginia. She was anxious to return to her husband and relatives. When the winter was well commenced a party commanded by Matthias Harman took her to her Virginia settlements and restored her to her husband and relatives. On the way the party was attacked several times, but succeeded in beating off the savages.[21] It was unusual to find Indians in the woods in the winter, and from this circumstance it was feared that they would prove exceedingly troublesome to the settlers at the blockhouse the next summer.

Mrs. Wiley was in captivity about eleven months. After her return she and her husband lived in Virginia about twelve years; they then moved to Kentucky, settling on the Big Sandy River just above the mouth of Tom's Creek, in what is now Johnson County, and some fifteen miles from the blockhouse and ten or twelve miles from the old Indian town at the mouth of Little Mudlick Creek. The Presbyterians had no church organization in that part of Kentucky, and she and her husband were members of the Baptist Church. Thomas Wiley died where he first settled in Kentucky about the year 1810, and Mrs. Wiley remained a widow twenty-one years, dying of paralysis in

---

21 The attacks made by the Indians upon the party which escorted Mrs. Wiley back to Virginia and the devices practiced to evade the savages would in themselves make an interesting story. It often seemed as though they were lost, and Mrs. Wiley had to bear a rifle and fight with the others, which she did effectively and with a good will.

the year 1831. They left a large family and their descendants live now in the Big Sandy Valley and are numerous and respectable.

The Indians attacked the blockhouse several times during the summer of 1788. The settlers surrounded it with a stockade. The Indians maintained something of a siege which lasted for about three weeks. This was in September. On account of their presence all the time no crops could be raised that summer. Several of them were killed by the settlers. Some of the settlers became discouraged, and as soon as cold weather enabled them to do so they returned to the Virginia settlements. Thus weakened it was not believed that the fort could be defended another year. The settlers all returned to Virginia during the winter of 1788-89. The Indians immediately destroyed the blockhouse. It was burned, together with some cabins which the settlers had erected in the vicinity.

In the winter of 1789-90 some of these settlers returned to the blockhouse site. They were accompanied by other settlers, a majority of whom were from Lee and Scott counties, Virginia. They erected a second blockhouse where the first one had stood, but it was not so substantially built as was the first one. In the summer of 1791 many new settlers came. The settlement was troubled much by the Indians for several years, but it was never again broken up. It is believed that Matthias Harman did not again settle permanently in the Blockhouse Bottom, though he was there for some years. He died in Tazewell County, Virginia. Daniel Harman became a permanent settler in the vicinity of the first settlement, and his descendants in the Big Sandy Valley are many. They are industrious, and are good citizens. Henry Skaggs and James Skaggs both returned to Kentucky. They lived for some years in the vicinity of the Blockhouse Bottom, but when times were settled they went to live on the head waters of Big Blaine Creek. Their descendants live now on Big Blaine Creek, the Little Sandy River, and the Licking River. The Leeks came with the second settlement, and their descendants are yet to be found on the Louisa River. The same can be said of the Horns. An account of the families which came with the settlers in the second colony will be furnished at some time in the future.

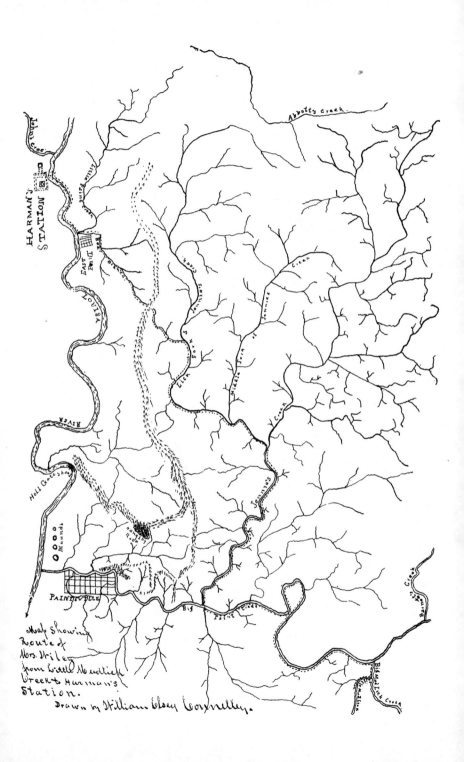

Map showing
Route of
Mrs. Wiley
from Little Mudlick
Creek to Harman's
Station.

Drawn by William Elsey Connelley.

CHAPTER X

I have believed it well to set out in an additional chapter other accounts of the captivity of Mrs. Wiley. It is not necessary to make any comment on them, for when they are read in connection with my account as written from the dictation of Adam P. Wiley the causes for any differences of statement will readily appear.

The adventures of Mrs. Wiley are related in every household in the Big Sandy Valley. I was perfectly familiar with them long before I ever saw Mr. Wiley. They are related now in a variety of forms, and like all traditionary accounts of an important event after the lapse of more than a century they differ somewhat as to details. The following account furnished me by my friend, James Hayden Van Hoose, of Fayetteville, Arkansas, is a fair statement of the tradition as it is briefly related in these days. Writing me under date of August 4, 1895, he says:

I have heard my grandmother tell the story as she received it from old Jennie Wiley nearly ninety years ago. Jennie Wiley was one of the early settlers in Western Virginia, and on a day in the fall of the year while all the men folks of the settlement were off on a scout, a band of Indians came in and murdered and plundered the people left at home. All her children were killed except her youngest, then about 15 months old, which they allowed her to carry with her into captivity. They took her down into Kentucky and kept her with them until in the early part of the next spring. Another babe was born which they allowed her to nurse for a few weeks, but becoming uneasy about some news brought in by their scouts, they killed both of her babes one night and dried their little scalps by the fire before her eyes. She saw that trouble was brewing and resolved to make an effort to escape.

After they were asleep she quietly stole away from the camp, traveling in the direction she thought would lead to the white settlements. All night she traveled, accompanied by her faithful little dog who had followed her from her home, and stayed by her all the time in captivity.

She reached the mouth of this little creek which empties into Paint Creek, and she followed it to its head. During the day a little snow fell, and for fear they would track her in the snow she waded in the water, but her little dog would run along the bank. To keep them from finding his tracks in the snow, she called him to her in the water, and held him under until he was drowned. She said she could not keep back the tears while drowning him as she thought of how faitfhul he had been to her. She said she passed through the low gap now known as " Hager's Gap," where my father afterward built his house, in which I was born 66 years ago and a portion of which yet stands. Traveling up a little branch, once known as the " Stillhouse Branch," to its head, she reached the " Limestone Cliff," at the mouth of the " Limestone Branch," late at night. She rested under the cliff of rocks and slept a few hours until daylight, when she renewed her tramp along the river bank, until she reached a point directly opposite the blockhouse, or rude fort. She called loudly as she could for some one to come over after her. The river was very high, and some of the women came down to the bank. She called to them to send some one over after her, as she knew the Indians were after her; but they answered her by saying there was no canoe about the fort, and that the men were all gone after Indians on a scout, and only one old man left with the women and little children, and he was 80 years old, and feeble. She told them to get some dry logs and pin them together and make a raft, but they told her there was not any auger about the place. Then she said tie the logs together with ropes. But there was no rope. Then she said " get a grape vine " and tie the logs together with that.

The old man and women got three dry poplar logs and fastened them together with grape vines, and got a board for a paddle. The old man got on the raft and shoved it from the shore. He finally reached the side where she was so anxiously waiting, and she got on the other end of

The escape of Mrs. Wiley from the Indians at the Falls of
Little Mudlick Creek

the raft and shoved it from the shore. The old man began paddling for the shore from whence he had come. The strong current carried them down the river some distance, and finally the vines began to come loose. The raft began to spread apart. The old man ceased paddling and fell upon his knees and began to pray, but Mrs. Wiley had more faith in " works " than in prayer. She seized the paddle out of his hands, and while he prayed she paddled, and succeeded in propelling the raft in under some swinging maple limbs that overhung the water. The old man grabbed hold of the limbs and pulled the raft ashore; they both reached dry land in safety. And none too soon, either; for just as they reached the top of the bank, three Indians came to the opposite shore, on her trail, and called out in a loud voice, " Whoopee, my pretty Jinnie! " But " Jinnie " was all right, for she had reached the fort, and the Indians not knowing that the men were all gone, were afraid to venture over.

The following is the account of the captivity of Mrs. Wiley written by Rev. Zephaniah Meek, editor and proprietor of *The Central Methodist*, of Catlettsburg, Kentucky, for Dr. Ely's *The Big Sandy Valley*. With the exception of the date this brief sketch is singularly accurate. Mr. Meek was familiar with the story of Mrs. Wiley almost all his life. I believe he was born near the Wiley homestead on the Big Sandy River.

JENNY WILEY

The most romantic history in the early settlement of the Big Sandy Valley is that of Jenny Wiley. This history we proceed to give from the most reliable sources at our command, drawing our facts mainly from Hardesty's " Historical and Biographical Encyclopedia."

There is hardly a man or woman in Eastern Kentucky who is not familiar with the story of the life of this remarkable woman. The facts of her capture by the Indians, escape from them, and return to her home, have been handed down from parent to child, and they are well remembered. Her maiden name was Jenny Sellards. She married Thomas Wiley, a native of Ireland, who had emigrated and settled on Walker's Creek, in Wythe, now Tazewell County, Va., where they were living at the time of the capture by the Indians. She had a sister living near by, the wife of John Borders, who was the father of the Rev. John Borders, a noted Baptist preacher, Hezekiah Borders, Judge Archibald Borders, and several daughters. Several families named Harmon lived in the same neighborhood, some of whom were noted Indian scouts.

At the time of the capture of Jenny, Thomas Wiley, her husband, was out in the woods digging ginseng. This was in the year 1790. The destruction of the Wiley family, as hereafter recorded, was a result of a mistake on the part of the savages. Some time previously, in an engagement with a party of Cherokees, one of the Harmons had shot and killed two or three of their number, and a party of five returned to seek vengeance on the Harmons, but ignorant of the location of their cabin, fell upon Wiley's instead.

John Borders warned Mrs. Wiley that he feared Indians were in the neighborhood, and urged her to go to his house and remain until Wiley's return, but as she had a piece of cloth in the loom, she said she would finish it and then go. The delay on the part of Mrs. Wiley was a fatal one. Darkness came on, and with it came the attack upon the defenseless family. The Indians rushed into the house, and after tomahawking and scalping a younger brother and three of the children, and taking Mrs. Wiley, her infant (a year and a half old), and Mr. Wiley's hunting dog, started towards the Ohio River. At the time the Indian trail led down what is now known as Jennie's Creek, and along it they proceeded until they reached the mouth of that stream, and then down Tug and Big Sandy rivers to the Ohio.

No sooner had the news of the horrid butchery spread among the inhabitants of the Walker's Creek settlement than a party, among whom were Lazrus Damron and Matthias Harmon, started in pursuit. They followed on for several days, but failing to come up with the perpetrators of the terrible outrage, the pursuit was abandoned, and all returned to their homes. The Indians expected that they would be followed, and the infant of Mrs. Wiley proving an incumbrance to their flight, they dashed out its brains against a beech tree when a short distance below where Mr. William C. Crum now resides, and two miles from Jennie's Creek. This tree was standing and well known to the inhabitants of this section during the first quarter of the present century.

When the savages, with their captive, reached the Ohio, it was very much swollen; with a shout of O-high-o, they turned down that stream, and continued their journey to the mouth of the Little Sandy. Up that stream they went to the mouth of Dry Fork, and up the same to its head, when they crossed the dividing ridge and proceeded down what is now called Cherokee Fork of Big Blaine Creek, to a point within two miles of its mouth, where they halted and took shelter between a ledge of rocks. Here they remained for several months, and during the time Mrs. Wiley was delivered of a child. At this time the Indians were very kind to her; but when the child was three weeks old they decided to test him, to see whether he would make a brave warrior. Having tied him to a flat piece of wood they slipped him into the water to see if he would cry. He screamed furiously, and they took him by the heels and dashed his brains out against an oak tree.

When they left this encampment they proceeded down to the mouth of Cherokee Creek, then up Big Blaine to the mouth of Hood's Fork, thence up that stream to its source; from here they crossed over the dividing ridge to the waters of Mud Lick, and down the same to its mouth, where they once more formed an encampment.

About this time several settlements were made on the headwaters of the Big Sandy, and the Indians decided to kill their captive, and accordingly prepared for the execution; but just when the awful hour was come, an old Cherokee chief, who in the meantime had joined the party, proposed to buy her from the others on condition that she would teach his squaws to make cloth like the gown she wore. Thus was her life saved, but she was reduced to the most abject slavery, and was made to carry water, wood, and build fires. For some time they bound her when they were out hunting; but as time wore away they relaxed their vigilance, and at last permitted her to remain unbound.

On one occasion, when all were out from camp, they were belated, and at nightfall did not return, and Mrs. Wiley now resolved to carry into effect a long-cherished object, that of making her escape and returning to her friends. The rain was falling fast, and the night was intensely dark, but she glided away from the camp-fire and set out on her lonely and perilous journey. Her dog, the same that had followed the party through all their wanderings, started to follow her, but she drove him back, lest by his barking he might betray her into the hands of her pursuers. She followed the course of Mud Lick Creek to its mouth, and then crossing Main Paint Creek, journeyed up a stream (ever since known as Jennie's Creek) a distance of some miles, thence over a ridge and down a stream, now called Little Paint Creek, which empties into the Levisa Fork of Big Sandy River. When she reached its mouth it was day-dawn, and on the opposite side of the river, a short distance below the mouth of John's Creek, she could hear and see men at work erecting a block-house. To them she called, and informed them that she was a captive escaping from the Indians, and urged them to hasten to her rescue, as she believed her pursuers to be close upon her. The men had no boat, but hastily rolling some logs into the river and lashing them together with grape-vines, they pushed over the stream and carried her back with them. As they were ascending the bank, the old chief who had claimed Jenny as his property, preceded by the dog, appeared upon the opposite bank, and striking his hands upon his breast, exclaimed in broken English, ''Honor, Jenny, honor!'' and then disappeared in the forest.

That was the last she ever saw of the old chief or her dog. She remained here a day or two to rest from her fatigue, and then with a guide made her way back to her home, having been in captivity more than eleven months. Here she rejoined her husband, who had long supposed her dead, and together, nine years after — in the year 1800 — they abandoned their home in the Old Dominion, and found another near the mouth of Tom's Creek, on the banks of the Levisa Fork of Big Sandy. Here her husband died in the year 1810. She survived him twenty-one years, and died of paralysis in the year 1831.

The Indians had killed her brother and five of her children, but after her return from captivity five others were born, namely: Hezekiah, Jane, Sally, Adam, and William. Hezekiah married Miss Christine Nelson, of George's

Mrs. Wiley on the River-bank opposite the Blockhouse calling for help

Creek, Kentucky, and settled on Twelve Pole Creek, where
he lived for many years; he died in 1832, [1882], while on a
visit to friends in Kentucky.   Jane married Richard
Williamson, who also settled on Twelve Pole.   Sally first
married Christian Yost, of Kentucky, and after his death
was united in marriage with Samuel Murray.   She died
March 10, 1871.   William raised a large family, and after
the sale of the Wiley farm moved to Tom's Creek, about
two miles from the mouth, where he lived until his death.

Of the children of Jenny Wiley, Adam P. was the most
noted.   In physique he was scarcely excelled by any man
in the Sandy Valley.   Tall, straight as an arrow, brown of
skin, slow of movement and speech, he was an attractive
figure to look upon.   He was known far and wide as
"Vard" Wiley, sometimes called "Adam Pre Vard."
Why thus designated the writer is unable to say.*   In his
early life "Vard" was a great fiddler, and carried his
violin far and near, to make music for the young people to
dance by.   But uniting himself with the Baptist Church,
he for a time gave up the fiddle and went to preaching.
His sermons were, like himself, very long, and he was very
zealous and earnest.   After some years in the ministry —
the number we do not remember — he gave up his calling,
and was often seen making his old violin ring out charming music for the young people at the log-rolling, house-
raising, or corn-husking.   He lived to a ripe old age, and
died only a few years ago, at his home in Johnson County.
Before his death he visited the writer, for the purpose of
having him write out the life of his mother as he would detail it from memory, but our business engagements were
such that it was impossible to comply with his request.

The Wiley family, descendants of Jenny, are quite numerous in Johnson; they are a hard working set of men,
and retain in their memory the heroic life of Jenny Wiley
as a heritage of priceless value.

The farm upon which Mr. Wiley settled, just below the
mouth of Tom's Creek, was known to all the old people,
far and near, as the "Wiley Farm."   About forty years
ago it was sold to James Nibert, who lived upon it until

---

* His name was Adam Prevard Wiley.   The name Adam was for Adam
Harman who settled at Draper's Meadows in 1748.   The Sellards and
Harman families intermarried.— *William E. Connelley.*

some ten years ago, when he sold it to Samuel Spears, who is the present owner and occupant.

As the writer was born and reared almost in sight of the " Wiley Farm," he is perfectly familiar with all the leading facts in the life of Jenny Wiley, during her stay with the Indians, and after her escape.

While they were camping on Mud Lick, some six miles above where Paintsville now stands, she said they frequently ran short of lead, and when they wanted to replenish their stock they had no trouble to do so, and in a very short time. They would go out in the forenoon, and after three or four hours' absence return with something which looked like stones. Then they would build a large fire out of logs, on sidling ground, throw the ore on, and it would melt and run off into trenches prepared for it; afterwards, as needed, it was moulded into bullets. But, notwithstanding the ease with which the Indians procured their lead, the whites have never been able to find the mines from which it was taken. Years have been spent in its search, and long pilgrimages have been made, by those claiming to be able to point out the place, but thus far to no purpose.

Were we to repeat all the legends that have been handed down from the days of Jenny Wiley, they would seem too incredible for belief in this age, when romance and hardships are not so intimately associated as they were then. So, in the preparation of this chapter we have confined ourselves to facts, leaving out the fanciful, which the imagination of the reader can supply.

That there are vast lead mines in the valley of Paint Creek, perhaps on Mud Lick, there is little room to doubt. That they have never been found, in view of the universal belief of their existence, is likely due to the fact that the people in that section do not know lead ore when they see it. The story of Jenny Wiley was abundantly confirmed by Indians friendly to the whites, in later days, but they would give no information as to the location. We are sorry we can not tell our readers where to find these mines!

I insert here the account written by H. Clay Ragland, Esq., editor and proprietor of the *Logan County* (West Virginia) *Banner*. Mr. Ragland wrote a history of his county in installments, which he published in his paper. While there are some errors in it, the history is very valuable, and in the publication of it Mr. Ragland did his country a great service. I recognized its value as soon as I saw the first chapter, and procured it all; I have it pasted in a scrap book in consecutive order. It is one of the best annals of the valley yet written. The portion given here is chapter five in the series as published in the paper.

HISTORY OF LOGAN COUNTY

By

H. CLAY RAGLAND

CHAPTER V

As early as 1777 Henry Harman, a native of Prussia, with his sons, Henry, George and Mathias, and Absalom Lusk, made a settlement in what is now known as Ab's Valley, in what is now Tazewell County. The place selected by them had formerly been occupied by Indian lodges, and a portion of the land was ready for cultivation. They were soon joined in their new settlement by John Draper, James Moore, James Evans, Samuel Wiley and George Maxwell, with their families, and thus strengthened they felt themselves in a manner secure from Indian raids, and their horses and cattle were allowed to run at large in the fertile valley. For awhile all went well. The crops were planted and the wild game so abundant in the valley was hunted, and peace and plenty was promised. Indian eyes, however, watched from the wooded ridge to the west, and on a bright morning in the early summer of 1778, Mathias Harman and John Draper were out hunting about a mile from the settlement, when, becoming separated, young Harman shot a deer and then commenced to reload his rifle. Before he had finished he was seized from behind by a stalwart Indian, and on looking up he saw several other Indians in a few feet of him, and he gave up without a struggle. The whoop which the Indians raised at his capture notified Draper of the fact and he hurried to the settlement with the news. Henry Harman and his sons Henry and George at once seized their arms,

and with Draper pursued rapidly after the Indians whom
they overtook, on what is now known as Harman's branch,
in McDowell County.   Harman and his companions at
once opened fire on the Indians, and when the fight was
over young Harman was a free man, and five of the Indians were dead on the field while the others had saved
themselves by flight.   None of the whites were hurt except Henry Harman, Sr., who was covered with wounds,
six arrowheads being broken off in his flesh; not extracted
until he had been carried back to his home by his boys.
Draper is said to have deserted during the fight, and on
reaching the settlement had reported that Harman and all
of his sons were killed.   Revenge is one of the strongest
characteristics of the Indian, as well as all other uncivil-
ized races, and doubtless the Indians who escaped with
their lives from the fight of Harman's branch, dreamed
of being revenged upon the little settlement of Ab's Valley; yet bided their time until the little settlement should
again feel themselves secure from attack.

The crops for 1779 had been scarcely planted and young
Mathias Harman was busy raising a company of Rangers
to join the patriots in the Carolinas, when in the early
part of the spring a party of some thirty Indians dropped,
as if from the clouds, upon the little settlement, capturing
first James Moore, who had gone to the pasture to look
after his horses, and with a savage whoop, bursting into
the houses, murdering the Wiley, Moore and Maxwell
families, and capturing George Maxwell and Jennie Wiley,
the wife of Samuel Wiley, and daughter of James Evans.
The alarm was soon given, and Captain Mathias Harman,
with about forty men of the company which he had been
raising, was soon in the saddle and ready for pursuit.
General Preston, who had about one hundred men in his
command was notified, and made a junction with Harman
the next day at or near the present site of Welch.   With
this force they pushed down the Tug River to its junction
with Levisa, and then down the Big Sandy as rapidly as
possible, keeping their scouts in advance of them, but
they failed to overtake the Indians; in fact they lost all
sign of their trail after passing the mouth of Jennie's
Creek, on Tug River.   When in about eight miles of the
mouth of the Big Sandy, at what is now White's Creek,

Mrs. Wiley at the mouth of Little Paint Creek (East Point) in her
escape from the Indians

the scouts reported a large force of Indians, estimated at a thousand warriors, in front of them, and rapidly advancing up the river. The men had not stopped to hunt on the march, and they were entirely out of provisions, and the forced march which they had made had jaded both horses and men. Less than one hundred and fifty men in a wilderness, more than two hundred miles from a settlement, fronted by a wily and savage foe, numbering more than five to one, and acquainted with every mountain pass in the country, by which a party could have been thrown in their front and an ambuscade formed, was indeed a critical position. To fight was certain death and even retreat promised but little else. Nothing else, however, remained to be done, and posting his most experienced men in the rear of his column, Gen. Preston and his brave men, chagrined at their failure in recapturing the prisoners who had been taken from Ab's Valley, set out on their weary retreat up the river. In the meantime a heavy rain had commenced, and the mountain streams were in places overflowing their banks, making fording at times difficult, while the soft and yielding earth doubled the labor of the jaded steeds.

The weary march was kept up during the night, but without incident. The next morning both deer and buffalo were in sight, but they were afraid to fire a gun lest their Indian pursuers might locate them and hurry forward, or worse still, send a column by some nearer route to intercept them. Arriving at the mouth of Marrowbone, they found the carcass of a buffalo, which had been left by the Indians on their retreat down the river, and the bones with what flesh had been left upon them, were divided among the men. A short distance above Marrowbone they came upon a gas spring which had been lighted. Here they paused for the purpose of resting their horses, and of roasting, as best they could, the meat and bones which they had found at the mouth of Marrowbone. Some of the men to satisfy their hunger, cut the tugs from their saddles and roasted them over the spring. After a short rest the gallant little band again took up their line of march up the river. Arriving at the mouth of Pigeon, they found that Charles Lewis, who had been taken sick on their march down the river, and left at that place in charge of two companions, had died. They hastily dug a grave and

buried him, but just as the last sad rites were being completed, scouts reported the Indian column but a short distance below. Examining the creek, and finding it out of
its banks and covered with driftwood and debris, they
concluded that it was dangerous to attempt to cross it in
the face of the foe, and leaving the old trail, they took up
their line of march up the northeastern bank of the creek,
hoping to find further up the stream where it could be
forded, a gap in the mountain by which they could return
to the old trail on the river. Arriving at what is now the
mouth of Hell Creek, they went up that stream, thinking
it would lead them to the old trail, but after proceeding
about three miles they found in front of them an impass-
ible barrier of stone and they were forced to retrace their
steps to Pigeon, expecting to encounter there the whole
force of the Indians. Every gun was examined and a
fresh charge of powder put in every pan of their flint-lock
rifles. On reaching Pigeon they were agreeably surprised
in meeting their scouts to learn that the Indians had gone
into camp at the mouth of the creek, throwing only a few
scouts across the creek on the old trail.

Gen. Preston then determined to follow the creek to its
head, intending to rest for awhile wherever game could be
found. A short distance up the creek and at the mouth of
a small creek flowing into Pigeon from the eastward, several elks were seen, which were speedily brought down by
the trusty rifles, and the party went into camp, picketing
their horses so they could feed on the wild grass which was
abundant. There were no signs of Indians during the
afternoon or night, and after partaking of a hasty meal
the next morning the command slowly resumed its march
up the creek. A hunting party under charge of Ben Cole
was sent on in advance for the purpose of hunting game
and fixing up a camp for the next night. This little party
pushed to the front, leaving a trail by which the main column could be guided, never leaving the creek until they
came to its head. Here they crossed over the mountain
and wended their way down a small stream until they
came to what is now known as the " Forks of Ben Creek,"
where they found both game and grass abundant, and
Cole, selecting it as the camping ground for the night,
made preparations for the command, sending a part of

The Indians on the River-bank opposite the Blockhouse. Mrs. Wiley had been taken from this point on the Raft a few minutes before

his men out to kill game. Gen. Preston on arriving went into camp, and next morning, having heard nothing further of the Indian force, determined to give his men and horses a much-needed rest. It was to him and his command a new country, and scouts were sent out in every direction for the purpose of finding out what they could of the surrounding country, as well as their distance from the old trail over which they had traveled. It was soon ascertained that they were within a mile of the old trail that led up the Tug River, and that they were really camped on another trail that led from the river up the creek. Scouts following this latter trail found that it crossed over a gap of a mountain to another creek which flowed into the Guyandotte River, and now known as Gilbert's Creek.

After resting a few days, Gen. Preston sent the command of Capt. Harman back to the settlements, and crossed with his command to the Guyandotte River, where, after reconnoitering the country as far down as the mouth of Buffalo Creek, and then after resting a few days and feasting on buffalo which were found in large herds, he took up his line of march for the settlements, passing up Huff's Creek by the grave of Peter Huff, which being recognized by some of the men, who were with Huff when he was killed, the command paused and refilled the sunken grave with fresh earth and marched back to the settlements on New River by the same route over which Capt. Hull had returned two years before.

Mr. Ragland places the date of the captivity of Mrs. Wiley in 1779. It is evident that this date is much too early; it is the year given me by Adam P. Wiley as that in which his parents were united in marriage. At the time of the destruction of their family they had four children. Mr. Ragland has the events and dates mixed in the treatment of this and other matters in relation to the history of the Big Sandy Valley. He fixes the number of Indians in the party at "about thirty" or "some thirty." He makes the pursuing party consist of the expedition commanded by General Andrew Lewis, and which was sent out in February, 1756, and which is known in history as the " Sandy Creek Voyage." He has the expedition commanded by General William Preston and Captain Matthias Harman.

THE CONNELLY FAMILY

EN DIEU EST TOUT
FIAT DEI VOLUNTAS

ARMS OF THE CONNELLY FAMILY

DR. HENRY CONNELLY

One of the first traders overland from Missouri to
northern Mexico. An explorer in Mexico, New Mexico,
Texas, and Oklahoma. Was long a merchant at Chihuahua. Appointed Governor of New Mexico by President
Lincoln. Born in Nelson (now Spencer) County, Ken
tucky, in the year 1800. Died at Santa Fé, New Mexico,
in July, 1866.

*[From photograph in possession of his son, Peter Con-
nelly, Kansas City, Mo.]*

THE CONNELLY FAMILY

The Connelly Family, we are told, is descended from Milesius,[1] King of Spain, through the line of his son Heremon. The founder of the family was Eogan, ancestor of the Northern Hy Nials and son of Nial of the Nine Hostages, King of Ireland, A. D. 379. The ancient name was *Conally* and signifies " A Light."

The possessions of the clan were located in the present counties of Galway, Meath, and Donegal. The Connellys were also chiefs in Fermanagh.

The names Connelly, Conally, Conneally, Connolly, Conneallan, O'Connell, and other names of Irish families, are derived from the ancient Milesian name — O'CONGHALAIGH.

The Connelly family is a Southern one in America. It has been our boast and our pride that it was one of the first families in the ancient and honorable Commonwealth of South Carolina. Thomas Connelly and his brother Edmund, and perhaps two other brothers, John and Henry, came from County Armagh, Ireland, and settled at Old Albemarle Point about the year 1689. This settlement was moved later, to become Charlestown, in the colony of South Carolina; it is now the metropolis of the state of South Carolina, and the name is written *Charleston*.

These brothers were men of fortune and affairs, and they obtained large grants of land from the proprietors

---

[1] *Genealogy of Irish Families*, by John Rooney, p. 420. Because of this descent the family belongs to that people called Milesians in Ireland. The Milesians subdued and conquered the primitive race in Ireland, the Firbolgs, the small, bow-legged, long-armed, red-headed, Irishmen of today. The Milesians have dark hair and eyes and very fair complexion.

of the colonies, one such grant embracing, it is said, a portion of the present site of the city of Charleston. It is said, too, that they never parted with the title to this tract. They engaged in town building and the purchase, subdivision and sale of large tracts of land in various colonies, but principally in Virginia and the Carolinas. They induced many Germans to move from Pennsylvania to the Carolinas, so the traditions in our family say, a colony of whom they settled on their lands near the present town of Camden, South Carolina. In this business their descendants were also engaged, and it became necessary for them to send members of the family to live in different parts of the country, especially in Pennsylvania and Virginia, to prevail on persons to migrate to their lands and towns in the Carolinas. And they engaged largely in traffic and merchandising by sea, owning vessels which plied between the different colonies and which visited the West India Islands. They also traded extensively with the Creek and Cherokee Indians.

In the Revolution the Connellys fought in the patriot armies of Virginia, the Carolinas, and Pennsylvania. They served under Washington, Greene, Morgan, Gates, Howard (of Maryland), Lincoln, and Charles Cotesworth Pinckney. At the close of the Revolution many of them moved to the West, and the family became still more widely scattered. There is a belt of them extending across Ohio, Indiana, Illinois, and to Central Missouri. Some members of the family settled at a very early day in the wilderness of Northwestern Pennsylvania, and many of their descendants are to be found there. Quite a number of them settled in Kentucky, in different parts of the State. Descendants of these pioneer brothers are to be found in Tennessee, Georgia, Alabama, Mississippi, Louisiana, and Texas. Indeed, there are descendants of this early family in every Western State and Territory. They remain in large numbers in the Carolinas, Virginia, and Pennsylvania. They have been exceedingly prolific, very large families having been the rule from the first. Conservative estimates place the number of descendants of Captain Henry Connelly, who, after the Revolution, moved from North Carolina to Virginia and from thence to Kentucky, at certainly more than one thousand, and possibly more than two thousand, counting only the living. The writer once had a list of thirty Connelly families in Eastern Kentucky, each of which had ten or more children. The name is now written in various forms, and there has been, of late years, a tendency to shorten it to *Conley*, all the immediate relatives of this author so writing it. Some of the Illinois relatives write it *Connelli*, and accent the second syllable. Taken all together, the Connellys have been men of fair fortune. They have been of influence in every community in which they have lived. Many of them have been possessed of fine literary taste — some of them fair literary ability. They have been ever in the advance guard in the spread of civilization over the West, and in a number of States they have been pioneers. In the Civil War they were divided according to the locality in which they lived, but they fought on either one side or the other almost to a man. Constantine Conley, the father of this writer, was in the Union army, from Eastern Kentucky (the Forty-fifth Regiment, Mounted Infantry).

One of the most distinguished members of the family was Dr. Henry Connelly, late Governor of New Mexico. He was born in Nelson County, Kentucky, in the year 1800. His father was John Donaldson Connelly, born in Virginia, and either brother or first cousin to Captain Henry Connelly, later to be mentioned herein. Dr. Connelly graduated in medicine from the Transylvania University, Lexington, Kentucky, in 1828, and went that same year to Clay County, Missouri, to practice his profession. But there forming the acquaintance of one Powell, an overland trader, he joined his expedition, under one

Stephenson, to Chihuahua, Mexico, where he became a
merchant. In partnership with Edward J. Glasgow, he
amassed a large fortune. He married a Spanish lady.
The War with Mexico, in 1846, made it necessary for him
to leave that country, and a large part of his fortune was
confiscated. He went to New Mexico and met General
Kearny and Colonel Doniphan entering that country to
annex it to the United States. He took part in their op-
erations, aiding them in many ways. At the close of the
war he settled in what is now Valencia County and again
engaged extensively in merchandising. His first wife having died, he married there Dolores Perea, widow of Jose
Chavez. President Lincoln appointed him Governor of
New Mexico, and to him, more than to any other man, belongs the honor of saving the Territory to the Union in
the Civil War. He died in 1866 from an over-dose of medicine. He has many descendants in New Mexico, and his
son, Peter Connelly, Esq., has long been a highly esteemed
citizen of Kansas City, Mo. Dr. Connelly was one of those
hardy pioneers to whom the United States owes the ex-
tension of her borders. For nearly forty years his cara-
vans were among the largest that annually crossed the
Plains over the Old Santa Fe Trail. He led a large party
from Chihuahua to Fort Towson, on the Red River, Choc-
taw Nation, now Oklahoma, in 1839. He spent the winter
at that fort, returning to Chihuahua in 1840. In this trip
he explored a large part of what is now Oklahoma and
Texas, and he marked out new routes for commerce.

Edmund Connelly, the youngest son of Henry Connelly,
is said to have married, in South Carolina, a lady named
Mary Edgefield. They left sons and daughters, among
them, Harmon and Thomas.

Harmon Connelly moved to North Carolina, where he
owned lands on the then frontier. Tradition says that he
there married the daughter of a physician named Hicks.
This Hicks, it is affirmed, had married the daughter of a

Scotchman who was engaged in trading with the Cherokees, and who had married a Cherokee woman; he seems to have roamed the country tributary to the Little Tennessee. Harmon Connelly appears to have been of an adventurous disposition, for it is related that he made several visits to the wilderness of Kentucky, one of which was about 1763.[2]

Thomas Connelly followed in the steps of his forefathers and dealt in lands and townsites. In this business he was often in Pennsylvania, where, it seems, he must have settled, as others of his family had done. Whom he married is not known, but in the light of recent reliable information it must have been a Pennsylvania Dutch woman. Our family traditions have always said that the Connelly family in Kentucky had a strain of Dutch blood, though as to the ancestor from whom it flowed we were never informed.[3]

Harmon Connelly and Thomas Connelly were in the War of the Revolution. Thomas returned from Pennsylvania to North Carolina and lived in Guilford County. He was getting old, but he served for a time in the First South Carolina Regiment, commanded by Colonel Charles Cotesworth Pinckney. His service was in the defense of Charleston, where he had gone to consult Colonel Pinckney, who was his attorney in some business growing out of land owned about that city by his ancestors. This service was in the winter of 1779-80. It is said, also, by the traditions of our family, that he was wounded at the Battle of King's Mountain, the following October, being there shot

[2] Before coming into possession of all these facts and when I supposed I had obtained complete information I believed Harmon and Thomas married sisters, daughters of this Dr. Hicks, and so wrote it in my application for membership in the Society of the Sons of the American Revolution. The family Bible of Captain Henry Connelly disproves this, and I had learned before seeing it, from the pension papers of the Captain, that this was an error.

[3] Uncle Edmund Connelly, son of Captain Henry Connelly, always said that his grandmother was a Pennsylvania Dutch woman. We never gave it credit until I saw the pension papers of Captain Henry Connelly.

through the body; and the above-mentioned Dr. Hicks is said to have passed a silk handkerchief several times through the wound — through the body — to cleanse it. The soldier died from the effect of this wound some two years later.

Captain Henry Connelly, the Revolutionary soldier, was the son of the above mentioned Thomas Connelly. He was born in Chester County, Pennsylvania, and came with his father to Guilford County, North Carolina, while yet a child, probably soon after Braddock's defeat. Thomas Connelly was a soldier in Braddock's expedition and was at the defeat. And it is probable that it was the expedition and its disastrous results which caused him to return to North Carolina.

THE CLAN MACALPINE

The Clan MacAlpine is believed to be the most ancient clan of the Highlands of Scotland. There is an old Gaelic tradition which says the origin of the clan was contemporary with the formation of hillocks and streams. The MacAlpines are descended from the ancient people whose successors became kings of Scotland for twenty-five generations. The war cry of the clan is "Remember the death of Alpin," alluding to the murder of King Alpin by Brudus after the Picts defeated the Scots near Dundee in the year 834. The seat of the ancient clan was in Argyllshire.

The Clan MacAlpine is one of the oldest families in the world with an authentic history. A daughter of this old clan — Edith MacAlpine — is the maternal ancestor of all the Connellys, Conleys, Connelleys, and Langleys, and many of the Salyers, Holbrooks, Stampers, Halls, McCoys, Grahams, Underwoods, Spradlins, Williams, Stapletons, Hamiltons, Jaynes, Hackworths, Caudills, McGuires, Mays, Patricks, Rices, Prices, Blairs, Webbs, Fairchilds, Robinsons, and many other Eastern Kentucky families.

The Clan MacGregor

The most famous clan in Scotland was that of Mac-Gregor. It claims descent from Gregor, third son of King Alpin, who ruled Scotland about the year 787, and the clan is spoken of in Scotland as the Clan Alpin. The motto of the clan is *"Srioghail mo dhream"* – "Royal is my race."

Sir Walter Scott found more in the annals of the Clan MacGregor for his famous Waverley Novels than in the lore of all the other clans of Scotland. Rob Roy was Robert Roy MacGregor, and the novel of that name is an account of the adventures of that famous Borderer. In his *Legend of Montrose* Scott finds some of his most interesting characters among the Children of the Mist, who were the MacGregors, this being one of their ancient names. In his history of the clan Scott gives much curious and interesting information about the MacGregors. He says "that they were famous for their misfortunes and the indomitable courage with which they maintained themselves as a clan. The MacGregors strove to retain their lands by the cold steel." They had extensive possessions in Argyllshire and Perthshire which they held by the sword. No other clan in Scotland ever did so much fighting for their rights or for their country.

The ancient seat of the Clan MacGregor was along both sides of Loch Tay, and in modern times they have lived about the old Church of Balquhidder, where Rob Roy is buried.

Next to the MacAlpine the MacGregor is the oldest of Highland clans, and these two are closely related, one being a branch of the other. The MacGregors are now scattered all over the world, and many of them have been eminent as statesmen, soldiers, scholars. They are often distinguished by a stern and haughty bearing, arising from a consciousness of having played a famous and honorable part in the wars of Scotland and the world, giving them a sense of superiority they are always ready to maintain by an appeal to arms.

We are proud of our descent from the Clan MacGregor.

Archibald MacGregor, of the Clan MacGregor, Highlands of Scotland, espoused the cause of Charles Edward, the Young Pretender, in 1745, as did his clan and his country. He was a young man of fine stature and immense physical strength. His clan was not in the battle of Culloden Moor, having been stationed at another point, so it is said in the traditions of our family, but he had been sent to the commander of the Pretender forces with despatches, and so was on that disastrous field. There he was dreadfully wounded, being left on the gory field for dead, and his body stripped by the Royalist looters. He, however, revived and with great difficulty and much suffering reached his own country. There he was concealed until he had recovered somewhat from his wounds, when he succeeded in escaping to the colony of North Carolina, where so many of his countrymen were then living. There he married Edith MacAlpine, the daughter of a Highlander who had also been in the battle of Culloden Moor, and who had with great difficulty escaped with his family to America.

MacGregor never fully recovered from his wounds. His daughter Ann was born February 14, 1756, and some two years later he died. His widow married a Scotchman named Langley, and by him had several children. Ann MacGregor, growing up with these Langley children, was, it is said, always called Ann Langley by her friends and acquaintances. Some of these Langleys moved from North Carolina to the Big Sandy region of Kentucky at an early day, and their descendants may be yet found there.

Captain Henry Connelly married Ann MacGregor. Neither the date nor the locality of this marriage is known, but it must have been early in 1774, for their first child

was born in June, 1775.   The family Bible of Captain
Henry Connelly had the following record, which I removed, and which is now in my library.   The Bible was
found in the Caudill family, in Johnson County, Ky., in
1902.   It was published in Philadelphia in 1802, and it is
not the Bible spoken of in the pension papers, in which the
date of his birth was recorded by his father "in Dutch,"
as he says in his pension declaration.   As he had a son
Henry he was Henry Connelly, senior:

Henry Connelly, siegʳ, was born May 2d, A. D. 1752.
>[In his pension declaration he says he was born
>in Chester County, Pennsylvania, and removed
>to North Carolina with his father.]

Ann Connelly, his wife, was born February 14th, A. D.
1756.
>[Her maiden name was not given, as it should
>have been.]

Edmund Connelly, a son of Henry and Ann Connelly,
was born June 2d, A. D. 1775.
>[I remember him very well.   He married, in
>North Carolina, a Miss Joynes.   He lived to a
>great age.   His home was at the head of the
>State-road Fork of the Licking River, in what
>is now Magoffin County, Kentucky, where I
>often visited him when a lad.   He said his
>grandmother was a Pennsylvania Dutch wom-
>an.   I have seen him at my father's house, in
>Salyersville, and have heard him tell much of
>the early history of our family, but as I did not
>write it down at the time, what he said became
>confused in my mind, and it has taken much
>labor to correct many errors into which I had
>fallen.   I was too young to fully comprehend
>the importance of what he said, and I had not
>then learned to write well enough to make a
>record.   I was at religious services held in his
>house in 1865, and he lived some years after
>that.]

Thomas Connelly, a son of Henry and Ann Connelly, was born 25th of January, A. D. 1777.

[He was my great grandfather. He was married in North Carolina to Susan Joynes. She was the sister of the wife of his brother Edmund. A number of their children were born in North Carolina. It is probable that they moved, with his father, the Captain, to Botetourt County, Virginia, where lived many of the Connellys, and after a residence of some years there, moved to Kentucky, settling first in the Indian Bottom, on the Kentucky River, at the mouth of the Rockhouse Fork, in what is now Letcher County, where their son, Henry Connelly, my grandfather, was born, in 1810. They moved to what is now Johnson County, Kentucky, and settled on the main branch of Jennie's Creek, at the mouth of Mill Creek, where they opened one of the largest and best farms in the county, which was afterwards for many years the home of Martin R. Rice, Esq., long the wealthiest citizen of Johnson County. From this farm they moved to a large farm at the mouth of Miller's Creek, near the Limestone Cliffs, four or five miles above Paintsville. This farm was long known as the Burd Preston farm. There Thomas Connelly died and was buried. My grandfather, Henry Connelly, there grew to manhood. Peter Mankins was their neighbor, and a good one he was; later he moved to Washington County, Arkansas, where he died at the age of one hundred and fourteen years. He came from North Carolina to Kentucky with the Connellys. My great grandmother lived for many years with my grandfather, Henry Connelly, on the head of the Middle Fork of Jennie's Creek, and she died there in the summer of 1875, aged about ninety-two. She was descended from French Huguenot families named Partonairre and Guyon or Guyan. Her uncle, Henry Guyan, is said to have had a trading establishment at the mouth of the Guyan-

The Blockhouse Bottom, in which was built Harman's Station. East Point shows in corner on bank of River

[*Photograph by Luther, Louisa, Ky.*]

dotte River, West Virginia, as early as 1750.
By some it is said that the river took its name
from him, though I am of the opinion that it
was named, because the Wyandot Indians
found it a favorite hunting-ground, in their
honor or for them, and was later corrupted to
Guyandotte.

My grandfather, Henry Connelly, married
Rebecca, daughter of George Blair, and settled
on the farm above-mentioned. My father, Constantine Conley, was born and reared on that
farm, and when he married he was given a portion of it — the Wolf Pen Branch — upon which
he built a hewed-log house, where he went to
housekeeping, and where I was born. My
grandfather died and was buried on his farm,
and many others of my kindred are there buried, including my great grandmother, above
mentioned.]

Peggy Connelly, a daughter of Henry and Ann Connelly, was born August 8th, A. D. 1779.

[Of her I have learned nothing.]

David Connelly, a son of Henry and Ann Connelly, was
born June 24th, A. D. 1781.

[Of him I have not learned anything.]

Rachel Connelly, a daughter of Henry and Ann Connelly, was born April 8th, A. D. 1783.

[She married James Spradlin, senior, who settled
at the mouth of the Twin Branches, on the main
branch of Jennie's Creek, at a very early day.
Spradlin was one of the pioneers of Eastern
Kentucky, and was a substantial and excellent
citizen. He left many descendants. I remember him well, for he lived to be almost a hundred years old. He was bowed with the weight
of his years, and after he was ninety I have
seen him on horseback, riding to Paintsville.
I helped to dig his grave, and my father assisted to place him in his coffin. So bent forward
was his head that the coffin-lid would not close,

and it was sawed off by my father so as to reach
only to his breast. Then the lid of the box
which enclosed the coffin bore heavily on his
head, when nailed on. His death must have
occurred in the year 1871 – possibly in 1872.
He died at the home of his stepson, William
Evans, who lived at the foot of the gap on the
road to Barnett's Creek, perhaps a mile from
the old Spradlin homestead, which was then
owned by Martin R. Rice. He was buried on
the hill across the Lower Twin Branch from his
old home. I am unable to say when his wife
Rachel died.]

John Connelly, a son of Henry and Ann Connelly, was
born August 8th, A. D. 1785.

[He married in North Carolina a sister of my
great grandmother, Susan Joynes Connelly. He
settled on Little Paint Creek, near where the
road from Paintsville to Salyersville strikes it,
and in this vicinity, also, lived his father, Captain Henry Connelly. Hairston Litteral, Esq.
(almost invariably spoken of as "Austin" Litteral) lived near this point for sixty years. The
descendants of John Connelly live mostly about
the Flat Gap, Johnson County, Kentucky, his
children having intermarried with those of a
settler named Jayne at that point.]

Henry Connelly, Jun[r], a son of Henry and Ann Connelly, was born December 1st, A. D. 1787.

[I knew him very well. He lived on the East
Branch of the State-road Fork of Licking River, in Magoffin County, Kentucky. His farm
lay above that of Jilson Prater, father of Jeff
Prater, now a wealthy banker of Salyersville.
I have been at the house of Uncle Henry frequently. He was quite old, somewhat corpulent, but large and erect. He was a kindly
man, but Aunt Polly was of sharp feature, sour
visage, and cutting tongue. I have not any
pleasant recollections of her. She was tall and
bony, and I was afraid of her, and think Uncle

Henry had a dread of her two-edged tongue.
I have not the date of his death.]

Elizabeth Connelly, a daughter of Henry and Ann Connelly, was born April 8th, A. D. 1789.

[I know nothing of her; am uncertain as to her
having lived to womanhood, though she may
have married and left children.]

William Connelly, a son of Henry and Ann Connelly,
was born July 8th, A. D. 1791.

[He was a millwright, and was drowned in the
ford of the Big Sandy River below the mouth
of Abbott's Creek, two miles below Prestonsburg, Floyd County, Kentucky. He was building a mill there at the time. The weather was
warm, and after eating dinner one day he and
his workmen went bathing or swimming in the
deep water above the ford. He was a fine
swimmer, but it was supposed that having so
recently eaten caused some revulsion of nature
when he had been in the water a few minutes,
and he sank and drowned before assistance
could be had. His body washed through the
ford and settled in a deep eddy below. His
men joined hands and formed a line reaching to
him and rescued him. He was unmarried, a
young man of great promise, and was sincerely
mourned by the settlers. He was buried on
the farm of my great grandfather, at the mouth
of Miller's Creek.]

Joseph Connelly, a son of Henry and Ann Connelly,
was born July 8th, A. D. 1795.

[I have no information concerning him other than
this entry.]

The above is an exact copy, excepting my comments,
with the difference that the name is uniformly written
"Connely." There is no "A. D." in the dates of William
and Joseph. The record is well written in blue ink, and
was evidently copied at one sitting from some other rec-

ord, for the writing is uniform.   The writing is not that
of Captain Connelly.   He wrote his name on the inside
front cover of the Bible, and the signature is in a fine, firm,
bold one, and the name is written "Connelly."   I took it
out of the Bible, tearing off the white lining-sheet of the
cover, and I have the signature in my library.   It is the
same signature I saw affixed to papers in the Pension
Bureau.   Each and every letter is distinctly and perfectly
formed, and the signature was rapidly written, as is evident from its appearance.   It is "Henry Connelly Senr."

There is no record of marriages and none of deaths,
except the entry:

Henry Connelly, Senr, deceased May the 7th, 1840.

On a leaf inserted in the Bible is the record of the
Hitchcock family, as follows:

John Hitchcock was born Jan. the 2nd, 1772.

Temperance Hitchcock, his wife, was born March 22nd,
1781.

Names and births of the above named parents.

Phebe Hitchcock was born Dec. 5th, 1798.

Margaret Hitchcock was born July 25th, 1800.

John Hitchcock was born Sept. 8th, 1803.

Parker Hitchcock was born Sept. 1st, 1805.

The date of the death of Ann Connelly is not given, and
I have not been able to discover it, but it must have occurred about 1830.   In 1832 (March 8th) Captain Connelly married Temperance Hitchcock, above named, widow
then of John Hitchcock.   The Hitchcocks were Quakers,
and came to Kentucky from North Carolina, and it is
possible that they there knew Captain Connelly and
family.   From the Hitchcock family here mentioned are
descended many of the Caudills, Pelphreys, and all the
Hitchcocks of Johnson and Magoffin counties, Kentucky.

Down to the family Bible from which the foregoing record is taken our information rests on traditions told in our
family, and not on written records, and later research may

discover some errors, though I am of the opinion that it will be confirmed largely, if not completely, for I have devoted much time to sifting the matter and gathering information. I was fortunate in knowing the old people of the family, with whom I talked from my youth up. The record of Dr. Henry Connelly, Governor of New Mexico, and of his family, is made from written documents.

Henry Connelly was a captain of cavalry, in the War of the Revolution, in North Carolina. The record of this service is contained in the declarations made in application for a pension, now on file in the Bureau of Pensions, Washington, and of which I made complete copies in the year 1902. These declarations are set out here:

State of Kentucky ⎫
County of Floyd ⎭ ss

DECLARATION

On this 15th day of August, 1833, personally appeared before me, James Davis, a Justice of the Peace now sitting, HENRY CONNELLY, a resident of Floyd County, and State of Kentucky, aged Eighty-one years, who being first duly sworn according to law doth on his oath make the following declaration, in order to obtain the benefit of the act of Congress passed June 7th, 1832:

That he entered the service of the United States under the following named officers and served as herein stated:

That he entered the service and commanded one hundred men as State troops of North Carolina (called militia) as the Captain thereof on the 7th day of July, 1777, for *five years or during* the war in the County of Guilford, North Carolina. His Colonel in the first instance was Colonel John Williams. Then under Colonel Paisley. Then by Colonel John Taylor. And lastly, by Colonel Billy Washington. This applicant's company was a Horse Company and was raised for the especial purpose of keeping down a daring Tory Colonel by the name of *Fanning* who had made several daring attempts in the neighborhood of Salisbury and Charlotte.* During the first year of the service of this applicant, by the orders of his Colonel, the company traversed and marched to Rowan and Guilford in order to keep Fanning and his confederates down. During this year, in the month of October, the company encountered his scouts and routed them with some loss. The general rendezvous of the Tories was in that region of the country called the Haw Ford on Haw River. These counties and the adjacent neighborhood was assigned to the applicant's charge by his Excellency, the Governor of North Carolina, in the month of June, 1778. This this applicant and his company continued to do during this year 1778. And that winter he and his company rendezvoused at Salisbury. The particulars of this year's service was only a few fights with the Tories. The war was raging in the North, whither that distinguished

---

* Fanning, the Tory, mentioned here was the famous and notorious outlaw of the Revolution. He was born in Johnston County, North Carolina, in the year 1754, ''of obscure parentage.'' The poverty of his condition was such that he was ''bound out'' for his support to a Mr. Bryant, who proved a cruel and perhaps brutal master, and Fanning ran away when about sixteen. His plight was so miserable that some of his acquaintances secured for him a home with a substantial citizen, John O. Deniell, who lived at the Haw Fields, in Orange County. He had the scald head and was not allwoed to eat at the table with the family, nor was he permitted to sleep in a bed. When grown up he always wore a silk cap — his most intimate friends never saw his head uncovered. When about twenty years of age he went to trade with the Catawba Indians, in South Carolina, and there accumulated considerable property. Up to this time he had been a Whig. As he returned to North Carolina he was set upon and robbed of all his property by ''some lawless fellows,'' whom he supposed to be Whigs. He immediately became a bitter and relentless Tory and sought every opportunity to wreak vengeance on Whigs indiscriminately and to injure the Revolutionary cause. He murdered, as he says, many patriots and burned their houses. He was bold and daring and succeeded in capturing Governor Burke, of North Carolina, whom he carried a prisoner into the British lines. He was the Quantrill of the Revolution.

At the close of the Revolution he went to Florida. He wished to return to North Carolina, but he was always excepted in bills of amnesty passed by the Legislature and remained, consequently, proscribed and exiled. He

and active officer, Colonel William Davidson had gone, and
all remaining for the constituted authorities to do was to
keep down the Tories, which were so numerous in this
region of North Carolina. During this year, 1778, the
men suffered much for clothes and every necessary, and
our forage master frequently had to press forage for our
perishing horses. Continental money was then one hundred dollars for one – for this applicant could not get a
breakfast for $100 in Continental money. During this
year, by order of the Governor, this applicant's company
was placed under the direction of Colonel Davie, who then
commanded the North Carolina Cavalry; but he renewed
the old orders, and my district still remained as under
my former orders.

Early in March, 1779, the Tories broke out with great
fury at a place called the Haw Fields, whither this appli-

moved to New Brunswick and was there a member of the local Legislature.
In 1799 he moved to Nova Scotia, where he was Colonel of the militia. He
died at Digby, Nova Scotia, in the year 1825.

Fanning was a man of ability and the local leader of the Tories in the
Carolinas. He was the man on whom the King's forces always relied and who
never failed them. It was a distinct compliment to Captain Henry Connelly that he was selected to fight Fanning and keep him down, and he seems
to have been able to cope with the daring Tory leader. Fanning says many
of his men were taken to Hillsboro and Salisbury and there hung by the
''rebels'' as he called the Revolutionary authorities. No doubt these prisoners were taken there by Captain Connelly.

Fanning wrote an account of his doings in North Carolina, and the book
was published at Richmond, Virginia, for private distribution only, in 1861 —
''In the First Year of the Independence of the Confederate States of America.'' The edition was very limited, only fifty copies of the quarto form
being printed. And it is probable that these were the only copies printed.
The copy of Colonel James H. Wheeler, the historian of North Carolina, is
now in my private library. It is one of the rarest and most valuable of all
American books. The title of the work is as follows:

''The Narrative of Colonel David Fanning, (A Tory in the Revolutionary
War with Great Britain;) Giving an Account of his Adventures in North
Carolina, From 1775 to 1783, As Written by Himself, With an Introduction
and Explanatory Notes. Richmond, Va. Printed for Private Distribution
Only. 1861. In the First Year of the Independence of the Confederate
States of America.''

cant and his company repaired and dislodged them with the assistance of Colonel Lyttle from Rowan, who commanded a regiment of militia. During this year the Tories were fast accumulating in Rowan, and this applicant's Horse Company was almost withdrawn from Guilford to that section of North Carolina. The Whigs this year took a great many Tories, who were all put in jail and confined at Hillsboro and Salisbury.

In the month of November, 1779, orders were received by Colonel Paisley from Colonel Davie, the commanding Colonel, to rendezvous at Salisbury to start to the South to join General Lincoln at Savannah, but about this time news arrived that General Lincoln was overtaken at Charlestown, and all were taken prisoners. General Davidson now raised several hundred men, and Colonel Sumner and Colonel Brevard had several skirmishes with the Loyalists, in which this applicant and his company actively participated at Colson's Mills. About this time at a place in the western part of the state (N. C.) the Tories had collected to a great number and we marched against them and [met them] at Colson's Mills. This was in the Month of May, 1780, as well as this applicant recollects. He recollects well that it was just before or about the time of Gates' defeat at Camden. During this winter and the fall this applicant's company abandoned his district of " protection " and under Colonel Davie and General Davidson opposed the passage of Lord Cornwallis through North Carolina. At the time of the approach of Cornwallis to Charlotte, under Colonel Davie the troops posted themselves to meet the enemy. On the enemy's approach the companies commanded by this applicant received the first onset from Tarleton's cavalry, and the firing became general on the left wing. The troops were commanded by Colonel Davie in person, and for three times we succeeded in repulsing the enemy. At length we had to yield to superior numbers. In this battle we had many men killed, several from under this applicant.

In December, just before Christmas, General Nathaniel Greene, from the North, took command of us all. This was in 1780. We all, by his proclamation and the orders of our Governor, were placed under his command, and assembled at Charlotte. From there this applicant was placed under Colonel Washington and marched to South Carolina, to Augusta and Ninety Six. After marching in a southern direction for several days news came that Tarleton was after us. We were all now under General Morgan, and a terrible conflict ensued at the Cowpens between Tarleton's men and the army under General Morgan. Here the Americans were victorious and took a great many military stores, cannons, baggage, and six or seven hundred British and Tory prisoners. This was in January, 1781. It was cold weather, but inclined to be raining during this battle. The company which belonged to this applicant was placed under a Colonel Howard, on the extreme right of the Division, and this applicant commanded a company in the center. Our company, when just about to catch up our horses, was hid about four hundred paces in the rear of the line of battle. [The enemy] fell upon us with great fury, but we were fortunately relieved by Washington's Legion that hastened to our assistance.

After this engagement we all formed a junction with General Greene, and retreated with him to Dan [River], and crossed over into Virginia, and remaining there but a short period, marched back to Guilford Court House, and this applicant actively participated in this memorable battle, and he had the mortification to see his men in a panic fly at the approach of the enemy; and although this applicant endeavored to rally them, it was impossible, and many even retreated to their homes. But this applicant remained and continued to fight until the Americans were thrown into disorder and confusion and defeated.

At this time, or a few days afterwards, this applicant being unwell, and his company broken, obtained a respite for awhile, which was granted him [by the Governor]. He remained at home and did not go with General Greene to Ninety Six. During this summer he did all he could to get his company to assemble. Their cry was "no pay" and their families required them at home. He then went from Guilford over to Virginia, and in September, 1781, he raised a small volunteer company for three months, to join General Washington at Little York [Yorktown]. Little York was, however, taken before this applicant arrived. He knew a great many Continental officers and Regiments, and Militia officers, during his service. In the month of October the term of service of the Company from Montogmery County, Virginia, just mentioned, expiring, he gave them their discharges, and he himself returned to North Carolina, where he received the thanks of the Governor and a Certificate stating his services.

This applicant knew General Smallwood, General Davidson, General Rutherford, General Pickens, General Sumner, General Otho Williams, Colonel Cleveland, Colonel Lyttle, Colonel William Washington, Colonel Malmody (?), Colonel Lee (from Virginia), General Goodwin, Colonel Howard who commanded the Third Maryland Regiment, Captain Holgin, Colonel Paiseley, John Williams, the Baron DeKalb, Colonel Brevard, and many other Continental and Militia officers that he has now forgotten.

He has now no documentary evidence in his favor, having forwarded his commission about six years ago by General Alexander Lackey to the War Department. It has never been returned to this applicant. He received a letter from the Secretary of War informing him that as he was not a regular he could not be allowed his [pension]. His commission was from the Governor of North Carolina. He has made search and inquiry for it for some time, and he believes the same is now lost or mislaid.

He refers the War Department to Henry B. Mayo, Esq., the Hon. David K. Harris, to Colonel Francis A. Brown, to Colonel John Van Hoose, the Revd Henry Dixon, the Revd Cuthbert Stone, the Revd Samuel Hanna, the Revd Ezekiel Stone, and Revd Wallace Bailey, to Andrew Rule, Esq., to John Rice, to Jacob Mayo, Esq., Clerk of the Floyd County and Circuit Courts. These can testify to his character for veracity and their belief of this applicant's services as a soldier and officer of the Revolution.

Sworn to and subscribed the day and year aforesaid.

(Signed)   Henry Connelly   [Seal]

Att: J. Davis.

We, Wallace Bailey, a Clergyman, residing in the County of Floyd and State of Kentucky, and John Rice, residing in the same, towit, Floyd County, Kentucky, hereby certify that they are well acquainted with Henry Connelly, who has subscribed and sworn to the above declaration, that we believe him to be eighty-one years of age, that he is reputed and believed in the neighborhood where he resides to have been a soldier of the Revolution, and that we concur in that opinion.

Sworn to and subscribed the day and year aforesaid.

(Signed)   Wallis Bailey   [Seal]
                           John Rice   [Seal]

And I do hereby declare my opinion after the investigation of the matter, and after putting the interrogatories prescribed by the War Department, that the above named applicant was a Revolutionary soldier (an officer) and served as he states. And I further certify that it appears to me that Wallis Bailey who has signed the preceding certificate is a Clergyman resident in the County of Floyd

and State of Kentucky, and that John Rice, who has also
signed the same, is a resident of the County of Floyd and
State of Kentucky, and are credible persons, and that their
statement is entitled to credit, and I do further certify
that the applicant cannot, from bodily infirmity, attend
court.

(Signed)   James Davis, J. P. F. Co. [Seal]

INTERROGATORIES

Where and what year were you born?

Ans. I was born in Pennsylvania, Chester County, on
the 2d day of May, 1751.

Have you any record of your age, and if so, where is it?

Ans. I have it in my Bible, recorded there by my
father (in Dutch). I have it now at my house.

Where were you living when called into service, where
have you lived since the Revolutionary War, and where
do you now live?

Ans. I was living in Guilford County, North Carolina,
where I had lived since my father moved from Chester
[County] Pennsylvania, up to the Revolution. I have
lived three years in the County of Montgomery, in the
State of Virginia, and the residue of the time I have lived
in this County – where I now live.

How were you called into service. Were you drafted,
did you volunteer, or were you a substitute, and if a substitute, for whom?

Ans. I was a volunteer, under the Government of
North Carolina, by an invitation from the Governor, and
[my command] were called State troops or Militia. A
part of the men under my command were drafted men for
eighteen months. A small portion was for six months,
and about forty were volunteers for and during the War.
I was called into service by a recruiting officer by the name
of Holgin, I think a regular officer. I made up my com-

pany and reported to the Colonel and went forthwith into active service.

State the names of some of the regular officers who were with the troops when you served, such Continental and Militia Regiments as you can recollect, and the general circumstances of your service.

Ans. I knew General Greene. I have seen General Gates at Hillsboro. [I knew] General Smallwood, General Davidson, General Pickens, General Sumner, General Otho Williams, Colonel Billy Washington, Colonel Lee, Colonel Howard, the Baron DeKalb. I have seen, in 1780, Captain Holgin, Colonel John Williams, Colonel Nat Williams, who commanded the Ninth Regiment North Carolina Militia in 1778, Colonel Paiseley, Colonel Buncombe, Captain Charles Briant, Colonel Brevard, Major (often called Colonel) De Malmody, and old Colonel Cleveland, Lieut. Joseph Lewis, Major Charles Anderson, William Boma, Ensign.

I was directed by Governor Burke and Colonel Davie to keep down Fanning in Guilford and Rowan. This this applicant did with one hundred men, a horse company. He served in 1777 in this capacity, likewise in 1778, and until the fall of 1779. He then joined General Davidson and was with him at the battle of Colson's Mills, where he got wounded. This was in May or June, 1780. He was at the battle of Hillsboro, and had nineteen of his horsemen killed on the field, and seven died the next day of their wounds. I was in the battle of the Cowpens, under Colonel Washington, in January, 1781, and Tarleton was defeated and we took his baggage and several hundred prisoners. I retreated with my horse company with General Greene to Dan [River] – went over into Virginia, and remained with the army until the battle of Guilford [Court House]. I was in that battle, and my men all broke very near at first charge, in a panic, and fled, and many went even home. When my roll was called at the Iron Works I had but a few men left. I was then taken in a few days afterwards sick, and was permitted for my health to retire for awhile from the service. This was in April, 1781. General Greene went to South Carolina, and I went over into Montgomery County, Virginia, to see my relatives, and I here raised a three months volunteer company to march to Little York. I marched them on to the Big Lick, in Botetourt County, in September, and waited for orders, but before I received them it was too late, and I gave my men their discharges. We all went home.

Did you ever receive a Commission, and if so, by whom was it signed, and what has become of it?

Ans. I did receive a Captain's Commission from Governor Burke of North Carolina. It was, I believe, signed by him. I gave it about six years ago to General Lackey, who says he sent it on to the War Department, he thinks. I have made search and cannot find it. It was never returned to me.

State the names of persons to whom you are known in your present neighborhood and who can testify as to your character for veracity, and their belief of your services as a soldier (and officer) of the Revolution.

Ans. I refer to General Lackey, to Colonel Brown, Colonel T. W. Graham, to Austin Litteral, to Jacob Mayo, Esq., to Andrew Rule, to the Revd Ezekiel Stone, to Revd Wallis Bailey.

Sworn to before me.

(Signed)   James Davis, J. P. F. C.   [Seal]

AFFIDAVITS

State of Kentucky } ss
Floyd County

Personally appeared before the undersigned, one of the Commonwealth's Justices of the Peace, Phillip William-

son, Senior, of the County of Lawrence, Kentucky, and
made oath that he is eighty-four years of age, that previous to the commencement of the American Revolution he
resided in Wake County, North Carolina, that he shortly
after the commencement of the Revolution moved to Guilford County, and afterwards to Rowan County, that in the
year 1777, in the fall season thereof, Captain Henry Connelly, now of this County, Floyd, was constituted and
commissioned a Captain in the North Carolina Cavalry.
I was then well acquainted with him, and he was appointed
to keep down one Fanning. I was frequently with him
in the next year in Rowan. This was in the summer of
1778. He then commanded the company of Cavalry aforesaid. I recollect to have seen him several times in Hillsboro where the prisoners were kept. And I also recollect
him and his company was in the service during the year
following, in 1779, for I well remember several Tories
his company brought in. In the month of February, 1780,
I left Rowan, and came over to Washington County, in
the State of Virginia. I remained there till May, and I
went back to North Carolina. Captain Connelly was then
out with his horse company under General Davidson
against the Tories. I do not now remember that I saw
him any more for some time. I, about this time, enlisted
in the service as a " Three Months " man, and joined General Greene. When we were retreating I again saw Capt.
Connelly commanding his company in the service as a
Captain. The Infantry was compelled to assist the Cavalry over the streams. He was in the battle of Guilford.
I recollect that I saw him a day or two afterwards in the
army. I have known him for a long time since the Revolution. Captain Connelly was a Captain of the troops
raised by North Carolina (not Continental). And further
this deponent saith not.

     (Signed)   Phillip Williamson   [Seal]
  [Signed by mark]

Sworn to and executed before Francis A. Brown, Justice of the Peace of Floyd County, October 2d, 1833.

Floyd County Court ⎱
August, 1833 ⎰ ss

On this 24th day of August, 1833, personally appeared before me, the undersigned, one of the Commonwealth's Justices of the Peace for Floyd County, Jonathan Pytts, an aged man, and now on the Pension Agency of Kentucky, and made the following statement on oath relative to the service of Captain Henry Connelly, who was an officer in the Revolutionary War. This affiant states that he resided in Rowan County, North Carolina, long before the War, and that during the year 1777 Captain Henry Connelly, who was a Captain of a horse company from Guilford arrived in the neighborhood of the uncle of this affiant, with whom this affiant then resided. His business, as he told us, was to assist us in keeping the Tories down. A great many Scotch Tories had accumulated under Fanning, and many about the Haw Fields, and a place called Cross Creek. He was, off and on, during that year, in Rowan. I saw him several times in Salisbury in that year. In the year 1778 he and his company still were in Rowan. He knew him very well in the year 1779, for he was, according to this affiant's recollection, all the year in Rowan until Colonel William Davidson came back from General Washington's army and raised men to go and help General Lincoln at Charleston, South Carolina. This affiant saw Captain Connelly frequently with his horse company in Rowan. And the next year, or the year after, this affiant again saw him and his company just before General Greene got to Dan. He was along with the army. This affiant does not know whether Captain Connelly was in the battle of Guilford or not, for this affiant had been sent on an express to Burke (now called Burke). He does not know how long Captain Connelly enlisted for.

He belonged to the North Carolina Cavalry, and how long
he served this affiant does not know precisely. He does
not know who was Captain Connelly's Colonel; if he ever
knew he has entirely forgotten. The impression of this
affiant is that Captain Connelly's horse company consisted
of one hundred men, but he does not pretend to certainty
about this fact. And further this deponent saith not.

(Signed)   Jonathan Pytts [Seal]
    [Signed by mark]

Subscribed and sworn to before Stephen Hamilton, Justice of the Peace, Floyd County, Kentucky, August 24,
1833.

Commonwealth of Kentucky ⎫ ss
Floyd County, to-wit   ⎭

On this [10th] day of October, 1833, personally appeared before me, the undersigned, one of the Commonwealth's Justices of the Peace, Benedict Wadkins, aged
seventy-four years, who being duly sworn on the holy
Evangelists, [deposes and says] that he was a resident of
the State of North Carolina, Rowan County, during the
Revolution; that in the year 1777, and 1778, he knew there
Captain Connelly, who then commanded as a Captain in
the North Carolina Cavalry; and I saw him in Salisbury
also in the summer of 1779. He was still commanding
his horse company in the service of the United States as a
Captain. Captain Connelly then, I think, lived in Guilford [County]. When the army was under General Greene
I saw him with the army once at Hillsboro; and he was with
the army in the retreat from Cornwallis. The last time I
remember to have seen him was after the battle of Guilford – the next day. He was then a Captain as he was in
1777 and 1778 and 1779. I cannot state how long Captain
Connelly served, but I know he was commissioned as a
Captain of Cavalry and served in that capacity for several years. When I came to Sandy [the Big Sandy Val-

ley] many years since, I found Captain Connelly here. Since then I have known him well. I recollect to have heard it asserted that he was at the Cowpens when Tarleton got defeated, but as I was not there, cannot testify to that fact. The Tories were very bad in the western part of the State, and Captain Connelly was appointed to assist and keep them down. I distinctly remember that he commanded one hundred men and they were all chiefly Dutch soldiers. And further this deponent saith not.

(Signed)   Benedict Wadkins   [Seal]
[Signed by mark]

Subscribed and sworn to before Stephen Hamilton, Justice of the Peace, Floyd County, Kentucky, October 10, 1833.

————————

[State of Kentucky ⎫
Floyd County]   ⎬ ss
            ⎭

The deposition of William Haney, aged seventy-five years, that in 1781 he became acquainted with Captain Henry Connelly of the North Carolina Light Horse. He was then commanding as a Captain in the North Carolina troops. When General Greene's army retreated into Virginia I remember that he was with the army. He was in the battle of Guilford, I well remember. I have known him many years since the Revolution, and I know him well to be the same man.

Given under my hand this 9th day of October, 1833.

(Signed)   William Haney

Sworn to before Shadrach Preston, Justice of the Peace, Floyd County, October 9th, 1833, and the Justice certifies that Haney was a credible witness, as had all justices with the other affiants.

————————

Kentucky, to wit.

The statement of Mesias Hall, aged sixty-five years, who upon his oath, states that he is a native of the State of

North Carolina, Wilkes County. That he recollects many of the events at the close of the Revolution. That he lived and was raised a near neighbor to Captain Henry Connelly, Sr. That he always understood from all persons that he served in the North Carolina State troops in that capacity in which he has stated. That he never was doubted by any person. He thinks one of his brothers-in-law served under him in the Revolution, who is long since dead.

  (Signed)   Mesias Hall
  [Signed by mark]

Subscribed and sworn to before John Friend, Justice of the Peace, Floyd County, Kentucky, who certifies that Hall was a credible witness. No date.

The attorney who made out the papers of Captain Connelly was Henry C. Harris, of Prestonsburg. He was attorney for the family for a generation. In a letter, in the files relating to the pension of Captain Connelly there is a letter written by Mr. Harris, in which he says:

"The old man is a Dutchman, and when I made out his statement I could scarcely understand everything he said."

His claim was allowed and he was placed on the Pension Roll of the Soldiers of the Revolution at one hundred and fifty dollars per annum, beginning 4th March, 1831.

After his death his widow, Temperance Connelly, was granted a pension, and in consideration of the inadequate allowance to Captain Connelly, she was paid six hundred dollars per annum. In making this allowance to the widow of Captain Connelly a copy of his declaration for pension was sent to the Comptroller's office of North Carolina for verification. Concerning his service, the Comptroller wrote the Commissioner of Pensions the following

LETTER

Raleigh, North Carolina.
Comptroller's Office
November 10th, 1851.

Sir:

I have attentively examined the records of this office for evidence respecting the Revolutionary services of Captain Henry Connelly, and I regret to say, unsuccessfully. A portion of the records are undoubtedly lost. The Capitol was burned about twenty years ago and many of the papers of this office destroyed.

In addition to this, I find a remark in the Journal of the Commissioners on behalf of this State to state the account of North Carolina against the United States, that Col. (afterwards General) W. R. Davie neglected to make a return of the Cavalry forces of this State under his command, and expressing strongly the difficulty which they experienced in making out the accounts of the dragoons.

The abstract of the Declaration which you sent to me contains the best history of the Revolutionary struggle from 1777 to 1781, in the Middle Counties of North Carolina which I have ever seen.

There are not five men in the State who could have written so concise and *correct* a history. I could not have done it, and I have studied the subject for ten years and with unusual opportunities for information. The names of officers, places and dates are all correct. Where did he get them from? For you must remember that the History of the Revolutionary War in North Carolina has not been written, (except Colonel Wheeler's history, now in press). Is not the presumption, then, powerfully strong that his statements relative to his services are also correct.

I hope at some future time to write a historical Memoir

of the period embraced in the Declaration, and will keep your letter to refer to.

Very Respectfully,

Your obedient Servant,

Wm. J. Clarke, Comptr.

The letter is now on file with the other papers, in the Bureau of Pensions, where I copied it.

Captain Henry Connelly moved to Rowan County, Kentucky, about 1835, but returned to Johnson County in a short time. He died May 7, 1840, and is buried in what is known as the William Rice Graveyard, on Little Paint Creek, not far from the old Litteral farm, Johnson County. The headstone at his grave is of sandstone, and it bears his name and date of birth; also date of his death.

Captain Henry Connelly was the founder of the Connelly family in Eastern Kentucky. No family ever had a more patriotic or honorable head. He was of strong mentality, as is shown by his remarkable pension Declaration, which he dictated at the age of eighty-one, and which is so highly praised by the high State official of North Carolina. It is said that he was a member of the Presbyterian Church, but that Church had no organization in Eastern Kentucky, and there he united with the Baptist Church. This was the Primitive Baptist Church, members of which were sometimes called the "Hardshell" Baptists. About the year 1834 there occurred a split in this Church in Eastern Kentucky, and at the Low Gap Church, in what is now Magoffin County, on the Licking River, three or four miles below Salyersville, Rev. Wallis Bailey led a secession which he named the United Baptists. Captain Connelly and his descendants followed Bailey, and most of them have been members of the United Baptist Church down to the present time.

The children of Thomas Connelly (and Susan Joynes Connelly) were:

Frances, born in North Carolina, probably Wilkes County, in 1800. She married Benjamin Salyer, who owned a large farm on Big Mudlick Creek, Johnson County, Kentucky, where the road leaves that stream to go to Flat Gap. There he and his wife died, and they are buried on the farm. He died of cancer on the lower lip. I have seen him often. His son, Hendrix, lived on the home farm; he married Margaret Williams. One of the daughters married Joseph Stapleton, and another married Edward Stapleton, brothers. A daughter, Christiana, married John Williams, Esq., and their son, Powell Williams, is a prominent citizen of Johnson County.

William, born in Wilkes County, North Carolina, in 1803. Died there.

Constantine, born in Wilkes County, North Carolina, in 1805. He married, in what is now Johnson County, Kentucky, Celia Fairchild, granddaughter of Abind Fairchild, the Revolutionary soldier later mentioned herein.

Celia, born in Wilkes County, North Carolina, in 1806. She married Dr. Isaac Rice, son of Samuel Rice, the first settler on Little Mudlick Creek, Johnson County. She left a large family of children. After her death Dr. Rice married Malinda, widow of Britton Blair, and daughter of James Spradlin, the pioneer who settled at the mouth of the Twin Branches, and who was mentioned hereinbefore.

John, born probably in Wilkes County, North Carolina, in 1808. He married Margaret, daughter of Noble Blair. He lived on the Lick Fork of Jennie's Creek. He had a large family, one of whom is James Hayden Conley, of Johnson County, a man of culture and ability.

Henry, born in the Indian Bottom, at the mouth of the Rockhouse Fork of the Kentucky River, in 1810. This point is now in Letcher County. He married, in what is now Johnson County, Rebecca, daughter of George Blair. He lived on a large farm on the Middle Fork of Jennie's Creek. He was my grandfather.

Thomas, born in what is now Johnson County, in 1812. He married a Miss Davis, sister to the first wife of Martin R. Rice, Esq., of Johnson County. He lived on Abbott's Creek, in Floyd County, where his descendants are yet to be found.

Nancy, born in what is now Johnson County, in 1813. She married Asa Fairchild, son of the Revolutionary soldier to be later mentioned. They lived and died on a branch of the Main Fork of Jennie's Creek, the first considerable branch from the west side to flow in above the mouth of the Twin Branches. They left a large family, some of whom moved to Lebanon, Ohio.

Susan, born in what is now Johnson County, in 1815. She married John, the son of Noble Blair. He was a millwright and was a fine workman. He built a mill in the Middle Fork of Jennie's Creek, on his farm, to which I have often gone. They left a large family.

THE FAIRCHILD FAMILY

The Fairchild Family, of Eastern Kentucky, was founded by Abind Fairchild, a Revolutionary soldier, born in Westmoreland County, Virginia, but from North Carolina to Kentucky. His service as a Revolutionary soldier was in North Carolina. In 1902 I made a copy of the papers in his pension case; these papers are on file in the Bureau of Pensions, and are as follows:

State of Kentucky ⎱
County of Floyd ⎰ ss

On this 18th day of February, 1834, personally appeared in open court before the Justices of the Floyd County Court now sitting, Abind Fairchild, a resident of Kentucky, in the county of Floyd, aged seventy-one years, who being first duly sworn according to law, doth on his oath make the following declaration in order to obtain the benefit of the provision made by the act of Congress of the 7th of June, 1832.

That he entered the service of the United States under the following named officers and served as herein stated. He resided in Wilkes County, in the State of North Carolina, when he first entered the service as a drafted soldier on or about the 10th day of October, in the year 1778, in a company of North Carolina Militia of which John Robbins had been appointed Captain. He met his company at Wilkesborough, in Wilkes County, North Carolina, and Captain Robbins not joining us, William Gillery, the Lieutenant of the company, took the command and commanded the company throughout the whole tour. William Sutton, the Ensign, acted as Lieutenant, and the Sergeant, whose name, to the best of his recollection, was James Lewis, acted as Ensign.

From Wilkesborough we marched down to Salisbury, in Rowan County, North Carolina, where we lay three or four days, and then marched out to the town of Charlotte, in Mecklenberg County, where we did not halt, but marched directly on to Camden, in South Carolina, where we halted and staid about a week. From Camden we marched and crossed Santee River at Nelson's Ferry, at the mouth of Eutaw Spring Branch. At Nelson's Ferry, where we lay one night only, we took the right-hand road and marched on to Dorchester and came near to Perosburg, the headquarters of the North Carolina troops. The South Carolina troops were there when we arrived. We encamped about a half mile from the town where we remained about six weeks. Colonel John Brevard was the commanding Colonel of the regiment to which his company belonged. From the encampment near Perosburg, we marched up the Savannah River to the Three Sisters, where we staid but a short time, when Captain Gillery and his company left the other troops and we marched down the river about three miles to a place called the

White House, where we went as garrison to guard a ferry on the Savannah River. But a few days after, his company left the Three Sisters. General Lincoln having under his command about six thousand regulars (as he, this applicant, was informed) came on to the Three Sisters and remained there but a few days. During our stay at the White House, Colonel Syms having under his command about two hundred Light Horse troops, came there and encamped with us one night, and next morning left us. Every morning during our stay at the White House a Corporal and six men were sent to the ferry as sentinels where they remained until they were relieved by another Corporal and six men more. After remaining at the White House, to the best of his recollection, about six weeks, his company was marched around a swamp called the Black Swamp, lying near the river, to a place called the Turkey Hill, where the company was discharged, on the 10th of April, 1779. His discharge was signed by Captain or Lieutenant William Gillery.

From the 10th of April, 1779, to the 1st of June, 1780, he was out as a volunteer on short excursions, receiving orders from Colonel Benjamin Cleveland, in what direction to proceed in pursuit of the Tories, and if the Tories should be too strong, to return and give information to the Colonel, so that he could go or send a force sufficient to take them. In these he was accompanied, generally, by ten, fifteen, or twenty men detached from the men under command of Colonel Cleveland. In excursions of this kind and sometimes in service under Colonel Cleveland, with the other troops of the regiment, he was in service a few days over twelve months between the 10th of April, 1779, and the first of June, 1780, in the counties of Wilkes, Burke, and Rutherford, but mostly in Burke.

In the last of June or first of July, 1780, he went as a volunteer and joined Colonel Cleveland at Wilkesborough, in Wilkes County, North Carolina. He was placed in a

company by Colonel Cleveland, the names of none of the
officers of which he can recollect. Colonel Cleveland had
under his command about two hundred men. We marched
on to Ramsour's about ten o'clock, A. M., the day of the
month not recollected, but he thinks it was between the
5th and 10th of July, 1780. When we arrived the battle
between the Mecklenberg troops and the Tories was over,
and the Tories had been defeated. He then understood
that in this battle about one hundred Tories were slain
and two hundred taken prisoners. From Ramsour's he
returned home to his residence, in Wilkes County, having
been in service about two weeks.

He next went into the service as a volunteer in a com-
pany of which William Jackson was Captain. The names
of the other company officers he does not now recollect.
Colonel Benjamin Cleveland was his commanding Colonel.
He joined his company at Wilkesborough, in Wilkes
County, on or about the 1st day of September, 1780. From
Wilkesborough we marched on to Krider's Fort, in Burke
County, North Carolina, where we remained two or three
weeks, and then marched up and crossed the Catawba
River at Greenleaf Ford, near Morgantown. From there
we marched to the head of Cane Creek, a branch of Little
Broad River. Between Greenleaf Ford and the head of
Cane Creek we fell in with the Virginia troops under com-
mand of Colonel Campbell. From here we marched to
Colonel Walker's old place (then so called) on Little
Broad River, and halted but a very short time, when
Colonel Campbell, whose troops were all horsemen, and
Colonel Cleveland, after raising all the horses he could,
marched on with what mounted soldiers there were, and
left the footmen, about one hundred in number, to follow
on with all possible expedition. From Colonel Walker's
old place, he, this applicant, marched on under command
of Captain William Jackson, and crossed Broad River
and went down by Buck Creek and passed a place called

the Cowpens. We then passed down Buck Creek some
distance and left Buck Creek and crossed Broad River
again at Cherokee Ford. We then marched on to King's
Mountain – arrived the next day after the battle, a little
after dark, at the encampment of the American forces,
about two miles from the battle ground. Colonel Fergu-
son, the commander of the British troops at King's Mountain, was killed and the troops under his command defeated, and, to the best of his recollection, about — hundred
of them taken prisoners. The battle was fought, to the
best of his recollection, on the 4th or 5th of October, 1780.

From King's Mountain we marched back to Colonel
Walker's old place and then turned back towards King's
Mountain again, to Vickerstaff [see *King's Mountain and
its Heroes*, by Draper, page 328 – W. E. C.] where we remained about two days. Here ten of the Tory prisoners
were sentenced to be hanged. Nine of them were accordingly executed, and the other escaped. From Vickerstaff we again marched to Colonel Walker's old place.
Here this applicant and six or seven other soldiers were
left with directions from Colonel Cleveland to bring on a
wagon which he had taken at the battle of King's Mountain, and the other troops marched on and left us. We
went on towards Wilkes County, and on Cane Creek we
met four or five men sent back to assist us with the wagon.
We then went on to Wilkes County with the wagon, and
he received a discharge signed by Captain Jackson for a
three months' tour. The time when he received this discharge he does not recollect, but he is able to state positively that he was in the service three months on this tour.

He next went out as a volunteer under John Cleveland,
a young man, the son of Colonel Cleveland, who commanded as Captain. He met the company at Wilkesborough
on or about the 3rd of March, 1781, and we then marched
down (there being about forty of us under Captain Cleveland) to the old Trading Fort on the Yadkin River, in

Rowan, and returned from this expedition about the 25th of April, 1781, and received no written discharge, to the best of his recollection.

He has no documentary evidence, and he knows of no person whose testimony he can procure who can testify as to his services.

Sworn to and subscribed the day and year aforesaid.

(Signed)   Abind Fairchild.

The Court then propounded to the said Abind Fairchild the following interrogatories, to wit:

1.   Where and in what year were you born?

Ans.   I was born in the year 1762 in the County of Westmoreland and State of Virginia.

2.   Have you any record of your age, and if so, where is it?

Ans.   I have no record of my age.   My father had a record of my age, but what has become of it since his death I do not know.

3.   Where were you living when called into service, where have you lived since the Revolutionary War, and where do you now live?

Ans.   I lived in Wilkes County, North Carolina, until about twenty-five years ago, when I removed to Floyd County, Kentucky, where I now reside.

4.   How were you called into service; were you drafted, did you volunteer, or were you a substitute, and if a substitute, for whom?

Ans.   In my first tour of service I went as a drafted soldier, and in all my subsequent service, as a volunteer. I never was a substitute.

5.   State the names of some of the regular officers who were with the troops when you served such Continental and Militia regiments as you can recollect, and the general circumstances of your services.

Ans.   These are as fully set forth in the body of the declaration as I am able to do from my recollection.

6. Did you ever receive a discharge from the service, and if so, by whom was it signed, and what has become of it?

Ans. I never received but two discharges that I recollect of. The first was given by Captain William Gillery, and the last by Captain William Jackson, both of which were lost many years ago, but in what manner they were lost I do not know or recollect.

7. State the names of persons to whom you are known in your present neighborhood, and who can testify as to your character for veracity and the belief of your services as a soldier of the Revolution.

Ans. I will name the Revd Ezekiel Stone and John Colvin.

The affidavits of Ezekiel Stone and John Colvin are attached to the declaration, and the Court certifies that they are credible witnesses. The Court also certifies that Abind Fairchild is a reputable citizen and that it is believed that he was in the Revolutionary War.

The claim for pension was allowed, and his name was inscribed on the Roll of Kentucky at the rate of $40 per annum, to commence on the 4th day of March, 1831. Certificate was issued the 27th day of March, 1834, and sent to Hon. Richard M. Johnson.

Fairchild, the Revolutionary soldier, moved from Wilkes County, North Carolina, to what is now Johnson County, Kentucky, in the year of 1808, and settled on Big Paint Creek. His home was near the Fish Trap Meeting House, a famous Baptist Church building some six miles from the town of Paintsville. I have not a list of the names of his children, but I know that many of his descendants live in Johnson, Floyd, Magoffin, and other counties of Eastern Kentucky. One daughter married John Colvin, mentioned in the pension papers. Two sons of John Colvin were in the Fourteenth Kentucky Regiment, Infantry, in the Civil War—Jehisa and Abind—in Company I. Abind was called "Bide" Colvin. I knew them and saw them while their company was stationed at Salyersville. The Colvin Family, in Eastern Kentucky was founded by John Colvin, and it numbers many families now—the McDowells and others. These are all descended from Abind Fairchild.

The eldest child of Abind Fairchild was Mary. She married George Blair, my great-grandfather, and they left a large family.

THE BLAIR FAMILY

There is no more honorable or distinguished family in America than the Blair Family. It was founded in America by two brothers, Rev. Samuel Blair and Rev. John Blair. They were eminent Presbyterian ministers, and the founders of the Fagg's Manor school which was the beginning of Princeton University. Samuel was pastor of the Old South Church, Boston, for some years.

Some of the distinguished descendants of these pioneer brothers are mentioned here:

Montgomery Blair.

Francis Preston Blair, Junior, the first Attorney-General of New Mexico, Brigadier-General of Union troops in the Civil War, and United States Senator from Missouri; his statue stands in the Hall of Fame, Washington, beside that of Benton.

John I. Blair, the railroad builder and millionaire, of New Jersey.

Henry W. Blair, late United States Senator from New Hampshire. In discussing the family and its descendants with me in May, 1910, he told me that his sister had spent much time studying the early history and origin of the Blair family. She found that a colony went from an ancient town in France called Belaire and settled in Scotland. The colonists were known there by the name of the town from which they had migrated; they were absorbed by the Scotch and the name of their ancient habitat given them as a family name – *Belaire* – and finally *Blair*. There are other origins of the family and name given, but this has historic support and also probability, and it must be admitted as the most reasonable.

Descendants of these brothers settled in Southwestern Virginia, and from these descended James Blair, the first Attorney General of Kentucky, and whose son, Francis Preston Blair, Senior, was editor of the *Washington Globe* and political adviser of President Andrew Jackson. George Blair came of this family, and was born in Lee County, Virginia. He and his brother Noble moved to Kentucky when young men, settling in what is now Johnson County. They lived for some time near the mouth of Big Mudlick Creek. Later, George Blair bought an extensive tract of land across Big Paint Creek from where Paintsville was afterwards built. He erected a large hewn-log house on the bluff opposite where the water-mill was erected by John Stafford, at the mouth of the Blackberry Branch. This he sold to the Staffords, after which he and his brother Noble bought all of the Middle Fork of Jennie's Creek, George taking the upper portion of the creek. Near the head of this stream, about seven miles from Paintsville, he erected a large house of hewn logs, where he lived until too old to look after a home, when he went to live with his youngest child, Asa, in whose house he died, on the old John Rice farm, on the Main Branch of Jennie's Creek. I was present at his funeral. A year before his death I taught my first school in that district, and much of the time I boarded with my Uncle Asa, and talked much with Grandfather Blair. He was a strong character, rugged and independent. He was, in his young manhood, of immense strength, and he loved the rude sports of pioneer days and always particiapted in them.

His people had been Presbyterians, but no organization of that faith being found in Eastern Kentucky, he united with the Primitive Baptists, and he followed Rev. Wallis Bailey in the secession which resulted in the United Baptists of Eastern Kentucky. Though a strict member of the church and an honored one, he would sometimes drink enough whiskey to make him boastful and "funny," which he always repented in great humiliation after the castigation administered by his wife in the form of curtain lecture, and which, he has admitted to me, he dreaded more than any punishment that could have been inflicted on him. The children of George Blair and Mary Fairchild Blair were:

1. John. Called, by way of nickname "Goodwood." I do not now know whom he married. I have been at his house when he lived on the Louis Power Farm, at the ford of the Licking River, where he once rescued Mr. Power from a watery grave.

2. Levi. Married a Miss Cantrell, whose family lived on the headwaters of Big Paint Creek. He was a shoemaker, and lived all his later life at the head of a branch of Barnett's Creek. He had a large family. I have often seen him, having been at his house many times. He was a sharp trader in horses and cattle, very thrifty, and of keen wit. Of these traits in him I could repeat a number of stories. His wife was a hypochondriac.

3. Britton. Married Malinda, daughter of James Spradlin, the pioneer who settled at the mouth of the Twin Branches. He owned a large farm opposite the house of his father-in-law, where he died and is buried. After his death his widow married Dr. Isaac Rice. I have often been at their house. Aunt Malinda was a good motherly woman when I knew her, and still retained traces of the great beauty for which she was noted in her younger days. Uncle Isaac was cross and disagreeable at home, being particularly aggressive and sometimes offensive in argu-

ment on religion. Aunt Malinda often requested me to come and remain Sundays, so that Uncle Isaac would talk and argue with me rather than with her, upon which occasions I was furnished with a surfeit of cake, pie, and fried chicken as an inducement to come again.

4. Washington. Called always "Watt." He married a daughter of James Spradlin, the pioneer, and lived on the headwaters of the Upper Twin Branch. I was often at his house, having been always very fond of him. He was a genius, intellectually the equal of any man I ever knew, barring none. He was a sort of rustic Samuel Johnson, whom, indeed, he resembled in appearance as well as in mental traits. He always ate with his hat on his head, presiding at the meals of the family much as a sovereign wearing his crown. He was brusque and contentious, often abrupt and overbearing, imperious, but he had a kind heart, and he was very fond of children. He exacted implicit obedience of his children even after they were married and gone to themselves, saying that such was taught in the Bible. He was, indeed, a patriarch, surrounded by his large family of married children, all paying him a sort of homage. He was quaint and droll, and his conversation was eloquent and as pleasing as any I ever heard, or saw in literature. I have sat for hours wrapped in a sort of enchantment by his fine discourses delivered always at his own fireside, for he never talked much in public His home was his castle.

5. James. I do not now recall whom he married. He moved to Minnesota when I was but a child, and from thence he went to Washington Territory.

6. Rebecca. Married Henry Connelly, my grandfather. She was a woman of fine mental endowment, very affectionate, thrifty, manufacturing in her home the finest cloth made in Eastern Kentucky; and in this art her daughters also excelled. I remember that she was greatly interested in the improvement of the breeds of cattle,

horses, hogs, and fowls. Of all these my grandfather had good specimens on his farm. She talked much, I recall, of orchards and the cultivation of crops, especially of cotton and flax. Her flock of sheep was her pride. I remember how white and clean they always seemed to me, and how she went among them and was followed by them seemingly in love and affection. No man ever had a better ancestor, and I remember her with reverence. She died of typhoid about the year 1861, and she is buried on the old homestead.

7. William. Also married a daughter of James Spradlin, the pioneer. Her name was Sarah. He was a very intelligent man and a Baptist minister. He built a mill in the Licking River, just above the present town of Salyersville, where he lived until the State bought it and removed it under the impression that the stream could be made navigable. Then he settled at the mouth of the Rockhouse, in Johnson County, where he died. He was rather impulsive, and I could relate some amusing incidents this quality developed during the Civil War. Aunt Sally, so we called her, was an excellent woman, but of an excitable temperament. After her death he married Edith Montgomery.

8. Noble. Married a Miss Stambaugh. Lived at the extreme head of the Middle Fork of Jennie's Creek. Left a large family.

9. Clarinda. Married John Stambaugh, supposed in Johnson County to have been the most polite and well-bred man in the whole world. His wife's society became irksome to him, and he lived for a time openly with another woman, whom he believed more compatible and more "polite." In his last sickness, however, her politeness did not prevent her forsaking him, when his wife sought him, took him home, and cared for him until his death. She never married again. They had one child, a son, Buchanan Stambaugh.

10. Mary. I can not now recall whom she married.

11. Asa. Married Mahala, daughter of Josiah Spradlin, and granddaughter of James Spradlin, the pioneer. Two children, Alamander and Ellen.

Henry Connelly and Rebecca Blair were married in 1830. They were given by her father a large farm on the head waters of the Middle Fork of Jennie's Creek. On this farm they lived until their deaths. They were members of the Baptist Church, United Baptists. Services were often held in their home, upon which occasions the whole countryside were invited to remain for dinner. I well remember these feasts, though I was often kept busy caring for the horses of the guests until I thought I should starve to death. My grandfather was a large man, but without any tendency to corpulency, and he was one of the strongest men in that country. I remember his feats of physical strength, performed in clearing lands, erecting houses, in conflict with the wild beasts of the forest. He was also of fine mind, though this was of a practical turn, and he never cared much for books. He was a fine hunter, and a collection of his adventures would make an interesting volume. When he was but six years old he went into the woods a few rods from the house. There he saw a large bear seize his pet pig. He ran to the house and got his father's rifle and hurried back, followed by his mother. But before she came up he had shot the bear through the head and saved his pet, which was dreadfully torn, but survived. On another occasion he went into the woods with his elder brother, Constantine, who, while busy about some matter, gave him the gun to hold. The elder brother was startled to hear the report of the gun, and called out roughly to know what he was doing. "I shot a wolf," said grandfather. And there was the wolf snarling and struggling in its death throes. He was but seven. It was necessary for the person who killed a wolf to appear before the County Court to get the bounty paid for the scalp. This was the cause of his first visit to a town, he having to go with his father to Prestonsburg, where his appearance in Court caused so much wonder, when his business was known, that it was impressed vividly on his mind. On another occasion, when he was no more than seven, some young men were chasing a deer with hounds. He believed the deer would run through a field just below the house. He took his father's rifle and concealed himself in a hollow stump in the field. Soon the deer came by, as he had judged, and he shot it dead, though it was running at full speed. This was when his father lived at the mouth of Mill Creek. His good markmanship once caused him to receive a severe whipping from his mother. He made himself a pop-gun of the common elder. One of the family flock of sheep, which had been driven from North Carolina, was walking along one of the logs hauled in to be used in building the residence, eating the moss from its bark. He shot this sheep with his pop-gun. The "wad" struck the sheep just back of the "knuckle" of the front leg, where there is no wool. The sheep fell from the log as though dead, for the ball had struck just over the heart. But by the time he was soundly flogged, the sheep got to its feet and ran away.

Henry Connelly was a good citizen, esteemed by all who knew him. I could relate an incident in his life which showed his good judgment, his justice, his humanity. It saved a man from a life of crime and made him an honest citizen, but as his children are yet living I will not write it.

The children of Henry Connelly and his wife Rebecca Blair, were as follows:

1. Constantine. My father. Born December 5, 1831. Married Rebecca Jane McCarty. Lived on the Wolf Pen Branch of the Middle Fork of Jennie's Creek, where I was born. Moved to Salyersville, Kentucky.

2. Celia. Died unmarried.

3. Thomas. Married his cousin, ———— Connelly. Died at the beginning of the Civil War, leaving one son.

4. William. Born in 1835. Was in the Fourteenth Kentucky Cavalry, and died at Lexington, Kentucky, of typhoid while in the service. I remember that Grandfather went there with a wagon drawn by oxen and brought the body home, stopping one night at our home in Salyersville, where the friends and companions of Uncle William gathered to mourn his death. He was unmarried, and his genial nature, cordial manner, bright conversation, love of manly athletics, made him a favorite over a wide range of country. In youth he met with an accident, cutting off the fingers of his left hand while making a wedge to split timber.

5. Mahala. Born in 1837. Married William, son of Josiah Spradlin, hereinbefore mentioned. They had two children, Clarinda and Mantford. After the death of her first husband she married Nathaniel Picklesimer. No children by second marriage.

6. Clarinda. Born in 1839. Married Jeremiah Hackworth, a soldier in the Fourteenth Kentucky Infantry. Lived on the headwaters of Middle Creek. Left a large family.

7. Mary. Born in 1841. Married Farmer May, but died shortly after marriage.

8. Lucina. Born in 1843. Married ———— May.

9. John. Born in 1845. Married Matilda, daughter of Morgan Long, of North Carolina, who lived a short time in Paintsville after the Civil War. He was the largest man in Johnson County, but not in the least corpulent. He was above six feet, probably six feet four, broad shoulders, and of fine form. He was a man of immense strength. Lives now in Paintsville.

10. Amanda. Born in 1849. Married ———— May.

11. Catherine. Born in 1851. Married Andrew J., son of Martin R. Rice.

12.	Cynthia.	Born in 1855.	Married Lewis F. Caudill.	He was a Baptist minister.	Both still living.	Have a large family.

THE BURKE FAMILY

The Burke Family is of Norman origin, and with the Butlers and Fitzgeralds, is ranked with the most distinguished of the Norman-Irish.	The ancestor of the Irish Burkes was William Fitz-Adelm de Burgo, who accompanied King Henry the Second to Ireland as his steward, in 1171.	The family was related by blood to that of William the Conqueror.	Two of them, Robert de Burgo and William, his half-brother, were with him at the invasion of England, and the former was afterwards created Earl of Cornwall.	In the reign of King John the Burkes obtained large possessions in Connaught through the rivalry and quarrels of the O'Connors.	Becoming powerful, they subsequently renounced their allegiance to the kings of England, and adopted the Irish language, dress, and customs, and compelled all the other families of Norman origin in Connaught to do likewise.—*Genealogy of Irish Families*, by James Rooney, page 458.

William Burke was a private in the famous Cavalry command of Lieutenant-Colonel Henry Lee, of Virginia, in the Revolutionary War.	This was the famous Light Horse Troop of "Light Horse Harry."	In our family there are many traditions of his adventures, his prowess, his hair-breadth escapes.	Once he was captured and condemned to death as a spy, but was saved by being allowed to escape in the night before he was to be executed by a brother Freemason, the acquaintance of whom he had in some way made, and who was his guard.

After the war he came to what is now Scott County, Virginia, where he died about the year 1795.	Among his children was a son, John, who migrated to Kentucky with

a colony of Methodists led by Rev. Alexis Howes, founder
of the Howes Family in Eastern Kentucky. John Burke
had a daughter, Lydia, born in Scott County, Virginia.
I have mislaid the date of her birth. John Burke settled
on the Rockhouse Fork of Big Paint Creek, where he
bought a large farm. He was a cedar-cooper, and famous
for the fine wares he made – pails, churns, piggins, and
other vessels. I have seen him, but he was very old, as was
his wife. They lived in a log cabin in the yard of the residence of my Grandfather McCarty. They must have died
in 1860.

THE McCARTY FAMILY

The MacCarthy, McCarty, or Carty Family is descended
from Milesius, King of Spain, through the line of his son
Heber. The founder of the family was Cormac, King of
Munster, A. D. 483. The ancient name was Carthann,
which signifies "Kindness." The chief of the sept was
McCarthy More, Prince of Muskerry, King and Prince of
Desmond, King of Cashel and Munster. The possessions
of the family were located in the present counties of Cork,
Limerick, and Clare. The sept comprised the families of
the McCarthy More, McCarthy Raigh, O'Donovan,
O'Keefe, O'Mahony, McAuliffe, O'Cowley, O'Curry,
O'Collins, O'Dunnady, McCartney, McCurtin, McCutch-
eon, McHugh, and O'Scanlon. The McCarthys took their
name from Cartagh, King of Desmond, A. D. 1100. Un-
der the Irish kings, and long after the advent of the Anglo-
Norman invader, the McCarthy family maintained their
princely prominence.– *Genealogy of Irish Families*, by
John Rooney, page 74.

Richard McCarty was born in Culpeper County, Vir-
ginia. He was a soldier under Braddock, and was at
Braddock's defeat. His company was raised by one
Slaughter, of Culpeper, and was under command of Gen-

eral Washington on the Braddock expedition.   In the War
of the Revolution Richard McCarty was Captain of the
company from 1778 to 1781, when it was in the Virginia
Line. .He died of disease about the close of the Revolution.   (See *Heitman's Register*, Washington, 1893).   His
son Abner settled in Scott County, Virginia, and some of
our family say Captain McCarty lived until about 1785,
when he died in Scott County, but of this I have no proof.
It is usually believed in the family that he died either in
the war or soon after he returned to Culpeper County.
Abner McCarty had a son Wiley, born in Scott County,
whose son, John, came with a second colony of Methodists
to what is now Johnson County, Kentucky.   There he
married Lydia, the daughter of John Burke, in 1836, and
settled on a farm given him by his father-in-law, on the
Rockhouse Fork.   He lived there until his death, which
was caused by inflammatory rheumatism about 1861.   I remember his funeral.   My mother had taken me with her
in her visit to him in his last illness.   He was a small man,
inclined to corpulency, with the Irish fondness for amuse-
ment and merriment.   He was noted for his sharp wit and
fortunate speeches in repartee.   He was a member of the
Methodist Church founded by Rev. Alexis Howes, perhaps
the first in Eastern Kentucky.

   The temperament, spirit, genius, of the Irish people were
strongly preserved in the family of my mother.   The love
and reverence for the ancient traditions, stories, fairy
tales, and lore through which fancy and the supernatural
were interwoven were a passion with my Grandfather Mc-
Carty, and all this, intensified and multiplied, was inherit-
ed by my mother.   Grandfather sang innumerable songs
of Old Ireland, and his stories of the McCarty banshee
charmed me and so frightened me when a child that I was
in terror when put to bed at night.   My mother sang many
of these old folk-songs to her children.   She died so young
that I did not have opportunity to preserve any of them,

CONSTANTINE CONLEY, JR.
Father of the Author
[*Photograph by Luther, Louisa, Ky.*]

but the spirit and rhythm of them so took hold of me that I hear always the music of them.

My Grandmother McCarty lived to a great age, dying a few years ago in Owsley County, Kentucky, but I have not the date of her birth or death. Children:

1. Rebecca Jane. Born January 14, 1837. My mother. Married my father, Constantine Conley, Junior, in 1854, in Johnson County.

2. Mary A. Married Rev. Samuel K. Ramey, long Presiding Elder of the Middlesboro District. No children.

3. Martha. Married Franklin Centers, of Clay County, Kentucky. They have a large family.

4. John. Married Sarah, daughter of ——— Burkett. Lives at Brazil, Indiana. Has two sons, Wiley and James.

5. Abner. Was made deaf and a mute by scarlet fever when an infant. Never married.

6. Wiley. Married Frances, daughter of Rev. Robert Calhoun, of the Methodist Church. Lives in Johnson County.

7. Amanda. Married James Estep, and removed to Booneville, Owsley County, Kentucky.

8. Angelina. Married Joseph Estep. They live in Booneville, also.

A sister of my grandmother married Rev. William Green, a devout and eloquent minister of the Methodist Church in Johnson County, and who was born in Scott County, Virginia. They left a large family, but I am not informed as to number and residence.

CONSTANTINE CONLEY, JUNIOR

Constantine Conley, Junior, son of Henry Connelly and Rebecca Blair, his wife, married, in Johnson County, Kentucky, Rebecca Jane McCarty, June 9, 1854. The marriage ceremony was performed by Rev. Alexis Howes, the venerable pioneer Methodist preacher of Eastern Kentucky. My father told me that when he offered to pay him a fee for performing the ceremony the old man said to him: "Young man, you could well afford to pay me a large sum, for I have united you in holy wedlock with one of the fairest daughters of the Church and one of the best girls that ever lived. I baptized her, an infant, and I have known her all her life. Her value is above that of rubies. I love her as my own daughter. Among the viands prepared by her own fair hands I will find a pie made for her wedding feast, and that is all the pay I desire or will have." This tribute I believe to have been deserved, and my father treasured it as long as he lived.

My father was the firstborn, and his mother had trained him to aid her about the house when he was a small boy. He was a fine cook. In those days the farmhouse was a manufactory where the shoes for the family were made. Those were days of homespun, pioneer days, the heroic days in the life of any land. In them was laid well the foundation of our government, and he that would have inspiration must study to understand them. My father was taught to make the shoes of the family, and these were made from leather tanned on the farm. This became his occupation in after life, and this trade he taught to me. His father gave him a farm on the Wolf Pen Branch, a prong of the Middle Fork of Jennie's Creek— a part of the old homestead. My mother was energetic and ambitious. When the County of Magoffin was formed and the county-seat fixed at Salyersville she desired to go there and see if opportunities could be found. They moved there about 1858, and built the first hotel there. For many years it was known as the Hager House; and it yet stands. Uncle William Blair sawed the lumber for it in his mill in the Licking River.

My father early enlisted in the Union army – in the Fourteenth Kentucky Regiment. But for some reason he was not mustered in that regiment. He enlisted in the Forty-fifth Regiment, Mounted Infantry, and served to the end of the war. My mother died in November, 1862. She is buried on the hill above where the mill of Uncle William Blair was, on a tract of land on which there was an old graveyard. My father married, for a second wife, Artemisia, eldest daughter of Caleb May, but she lived but a few months. He then married Charlotte Picklesimer, a niece of Louis Power, and a granddaughter of William Prater, one of the first settlers of that region. After the war he moved to Johnson County, where he lived until his death, in 1904. He died at East Point, and is buried there. Children:

1. William Elsey. Born on the Wolf Pen Branch, Johnson County, Kentucky, March 15, 1855. The name ''Elsey'' was given me by my mother for an old Virginia family with whom her family was connected by blood, but in what degree I do not know. The Sweatnam and Litteral families of Eastern Kentucky are also connected with this old Virginia family. I remember many things which occurred at the home of my birth, one of which I will relate. There was some game then, and my father was an expert hunter. There was an immense turkey in the forest about our home that had often been shot at by the old hunters, but he was so wary that all the shots had to be from long distances, and he had always escaped. One evening, at dusk, my father came in from a hunt, and I heard him tell my mother that the big turkey had just flown into the top of a large poplar that stood at the back of our fields, there to roost for the night. He said he would go out there at daylight and try to get a shot at him. I immediately set up an outcry to be taken along, which was finally, at my mother's solicitation, agreed to. I remember that it was not light when we set out, but the distance

was not more than a quarter of a mile. I was left at the fence, beyond which there was a thicket in which the big poplar grew. I could see the turkey outlined against the sky, and he was stretching his neck downward as far as he could, apparently seeking a place to fly down to, for it was dark below. My father must have seen that the turkey was intent on flying down, for he shot, as he said, before it was light enough to get a good "bead" on him. But it was a lucky shot, though one that came near missing. The turkey's neck was shot in-two at the body. Here he came flopping down from the height of a hundred feet and fell in the thicket very near me. I remember with what pride my father carried him home and exhibited him to my mother. The parents of both my father and mother were invited to come to a dinner when he was roasted. I remember seeing my mother roasting the turkey in a large iron kettle used usually for laundry purposes. I am not sure I remember the weight of the turkey accurately, but thirty-nine pounds always seems to me to be the weight. While I have a perfect recollection of seeing the turkey cooked, I have none whatever of the dinner nor of either of my grandfathers or grandmothers, though I have been told all were present.

2. Henry Clay Harris. Born October 18, 1856.

3. Louisa Elizabeth. Born May 26, 1858.

4. Martha Ellen. Born July 19, 1860.

5. John Mason. Born May 5, 1862.

Children by Charlotte Picklesimer, the third wife:

1. James Mason Brown. Born November 20, 1865. This is the date I have, but I am certain that it should be 1866.

2. Joseph Milton. Born April 28, 1868.

3. Sarah. Born August 29, 1870.

4. Mary. Born June 5, 1873.

5. Susan. Born June 11, 1875.

Constantine Conley, Jr., standing on the exact site of the Blockhouse of Harman's Station

[*Photograph by Luther, Louisa, Ky.*]

Having traced the family from the beginning to a point where all descendants can easily discern their particular branches and continue them, I cease at this point.   Our family, and all the families with which it has intermarried, are of the pioneer stock of America.   They are neither better nor worse than the other pioneer American families.   Pride of ancestry is an inspiration, and we of the South have it in large degree.   But it should not degenerate into arrogance or intolerance.

JOHN WESLEY LANGLEY

John Wesley Langley was born near the close of the Civil War, in Floyd County, Kentucky. He is descended from the Langley Family of North Carolina and the Robinson Family of Virginia, both old Revolutionary families. On his mother's side he is descended from the Salmons and Click families of Virginia and Kentucky. His maternal ancestor was Edith MacAlpine, who married Archibald MacGregor, and, afterwards, —— Langley. Her daughter, Ann MacGregor, married Captain Henry Connelly. John W. Langley, therefore, is descended from the Clan MacAlpine, the first of the Scottish Highland clans. And he and all the Langleys of his family are cousins to the descendants of Captain Henry Connelly — making, perhaps, the largest blood-relationship in Eastern Kentucky. Through his mother's line he inherits a large element of German blood.

Langley was educated in the common schools of Floyd County, and in the Georgetown, Columbian, and National Universities of Washington City, at which he attended at night while holding a government position. He won the first honors in all three of these Universities and took the degrees of A. B., LL. B., and LL. M., Doctor of Civil Law and Master of Diplomacy. He, therefore, has taken the highest working degrees conferred by any University in the country. His early education was secured with the usual difficulties encountered by a country boy in the mountains of Kentucky, and almost entirely through his own unaided efforts.

At the age of sixteen Langley was granted a teacher's certificate, receiving the highest rating in the county. He

JOHN WESLEY LANGLEY

taught school for three years, and was then appointed to a clerkship in Washington. Later, he returned to Kentucky and was twice elected to the Legislature of that State, receiving at the beginning of his second term the caucus nomination of his party for Speaker of the House, which made him the minority leader of that body. He afterwards was appointed a member of the Board of Pension Appeals, having received the highest rating of all who took the examination for the position; and the Secretary of the Interior, in one of his official reports, said that Langley stood at the head of the list for amount of work accomplished.

After holding this position for some time Langley returned again to his native State and was the nominee of his party for Member of Congress. The district was overwhelmingly Democratic, and he was defeated. He was then given the position of Appointment Clerk of the Census Office, and, later, the office of Disbursing Clerk was, by Act of Congress, combined with that of Appointment Clerk, and he held both positions until he was given his second nomination for Congress, in his home district, in 1906. In this position he made an exceptional record, and his salary was twice increased by special Act of Congress.

While his district had been Democratic by a good margin, Langley was elected to Congress in 1906 by a majority of nearly one thousand. In Congress he at once took high rank, and his record was so satisfactory to the people that, two years later, he was re-elected by a majority of almost three thousand. He is at this time, 1910, the unanimous nominee of the Republican party in his district for a third term in Congress.

In Congress Langley has been particularly active in his efforts to secure additional pension legislation, appropriations for the erection of public buildings and the improvement of the Kentucky and Big Sandy rivers, and Federal aid in the construction of public highways.

Langley has been a delegate to two Republican National Conventions, and he was the first to propose Roosevelt for Vice-President on the floor of the convention at Philadelphia in 1900. He is forceful, tactful, energetic, of a pleasing personality, ambitious to accomplish things for his people and the country, of the highest integrity and sense of honor, and a man in whom the people repose the fullest measure of confidence.

MILTON FORREST CONLEY
Editor and Banker, Louisa, Ky.

MILTON FORREST CONLEY

Milton Forrest Conley (spelling of name changed from *Connelly* by his father) was born June 13, 1868, at Louisa, Lawrence County, Kentucky, where he now lives. He is a great-great grandson of Captain Henry Connelly, of the Revolution, through the soldier's son Thomas and through Constantine, the eldest son of Thomas.

Milton Forrest Conley is the eldest of three children (two sons and a daughter) of Asa Johnson Conley and Elizabeth Leslie Conley. The other son is Martin Leslie Conley, General Manager of the Ohio & Kentucky Railway Company and President of the Morgan County National Bank at Cannel City, Ky.

Milton Forrest Conley was educated in the common schools, and in his sixteenth year established the *Big Sandy News*, a weekly newspaper since continuously published by him. It was the first weekly newspaper in Kentucky to install a linotype machine. During the years 1901 and 1902 he was a one-half owner in the Ashland, (Ky.), *Daily Independent*, the Catlettsburg, (Ky.), *Daily Press*, and the *Kentucky Democrat*, dividing his time between these and the *Big Sandy News*. He has been a member of the Kentucky Press Association for twenty-two years and an Executive Committeeman several terms; and he has attended the National Editorial Association four years as Delegate from Kentucky. In 1893 he was appointed Postmaster at Louisa and served four years. In 1904 the Louisa National Bank was organized with a capital of $50,000, and he was offered the position of Director and Cashier, which he accepted and still holds. He is identified with other business enterprises in the Big

Sandy Valley, and is one of the two Trustees of the Kentucky Normal College, at Louisa, which has four hundred boarding students and a like number of local students. He was married to Miss Willie Burgess in 1894, and of this union three children have been born.

ANNOUNCEMENT

This volume is the first of a series which I intend to publish on the history and genealogy of Eastern Kentucky.

Eastern Kentucky has a history as important and interesting as has any part of America, and it is my design to set it down faithfully in these volumes.

As shown in this volume, the people of Eastern Kentucky are descended from the best families of Europe and America. The only trouble has been that they have not made any effort to collect and preserve family annals and traditions. To gather authentic information about the early history of a family is extremely expensive, and this has been the principal cause of delay in securing it by some families.

I have extensive records of the Mayo, Leslie, Auxier, Hager, Meek, Cecil, Preston, Brown, Harris, Dixon, Witten, Patrick, Prater, May, Stafford, Mankins, Porter, Hanna, Rice, Rule, Price, Caudill, Adams, Gardner, Howard, Williams, Salyer, and many other pioneer families of Eastern Kentucky. I hope to treat these, or some of them, at least, even more extensively and thoroughly than I have the Connelly and other families in this volume.

WILLIAM ELSEY CONNELLEY

INDEX

INDEX

French, the: with Indians, built cabins at the mouth of Big Paint Creek, 55.

Friend, John: Justice of the Peace, 123.

GALWAY: County of in Ireland, seat of ancient Connelly Family, 95.

Gates, General Horatio: the Connellys served under in Revolution, 96.

Genealogy of Irish Families: by Rooney, referred to, 95, 142, 143.

Gillery, Lieut. William: acted as Captain of Abind Fairchild's company, 128; discharged men at Turkey Hill, 129.

Gist, Christopher: entry in Journal of referred to, 10.

Glasgow, Edward J.: partner of Dr. Henry Connelly in Mexico, 98.

Goodwin, General: known by Captain Henry Connelly, 114.

Grahams, the: many of descended from Edith MacAlpine, 100.

Graham, Colonel T. W.: referred to by Captain Henry Connelly, 118.

Great Flat Top Mountain: Indian trail ran along the top of, 41; sometimes called Indian Ridge, 42.

Green, Rev. William: mentioned, 145.

Greene, General Nathaniel: the Connellys served under in the Revolution, 96; in command of the troops of the Carolinas; great retreat of, 113; Captain Henry Connelly with on famous retreat to Dan River, 117.

Greenleaf Ford: on the Catawba; troops crossed at on King's Mountain campaign, 130.

Guilford Court House: battle of, 113; Captain Henry Connelly at battle of, 117.

Guyan, Henry: said to have had trading post at mouth of Guyandotte River in 1750; the uncle of

Susan Joynes, 104; Guyandotte River said to have been named for, 105.

Guyandotte River: origin of name of, 105.

HACKWORTHS, the: many of descended from Edith MacAlpine, 100.

Hackworth, Jeremiah: in the Fourteenth Kentucky Infantry; married Clarinda Conley, 141.

Hager Hill: mention of, 55.

Hale, John P.: work of referred to, 9.

Half-King, the: chief of the Wyandots; succeeded by Tarhe, the Crane, 11.

Halls, the: many of descended from Edith MacAlpine, 108.

Hall, Mesias: affidavit of for Captain Henry Connelly, 122.

Hamiltons, the: many of descended from Edith MacAlpine, 100.

Hamilton, Stephen: Justice of the Peace, 121.

Haney, William: affidavit of for Captain Henry Connelly, 122.

Hanging Rock: view of from Paintsville, Ky., 55.

Hanks, John: in the settlement at Vancouver's post, 68; affidavit of concerning post, 69.

Hanna, Rev. Samuel: referred to by Captain Henry Connelly, 115.

Hardesty's Historical and Biographical Encyclopedia: referred to, 81.

Harman's Station: shown on Imlay's Map of Kentucky, 1793, see map; cause of founding of, 5; some of the founders, 6; first cabin built on site of as early as 1755; probably the oldest settlement in Kentucky; had no aid from any stae, 7; site of fixed; blockhouse built at described, 67; dates fixed beyond doubt; shown on Imlay's